KU-395-930

FELLOWSHIP OF FREEDOM

EDENDERRY

2 0 APR 2023

WITHDRAWN

"An Irish Volunteer
Taking Liberty under
his Protection" 1786

FELLOWSHIP
OF
FREEDOM

THE UNITED IRISHMEN AND 1798

KEVIN WHELAN

Companion Volume to the

Bicentenary Exhibition by

The National Library and

The National Museum of Ireland

at Collins Barracks, Dublin 1998

CORK UNIVERSITY PRESS

A Note on Contributors

Professor Kevin Whelan is Michael J. Smurfit Director of the Dublin Centre of Irish Studies, Notre Dame University.

Photography and digital origination by Eugene P. Hogan of the National Library of Ireland.

Additional photography by Valerie Dowling of the National Museum of Ireland.

All illustrations are courtesy of the National Library of Ireland unless othewise stated. All objects in chapter IX are courtesy of the National Museum of Ireland unless otherwise stated.

Cartography and design by Dr Matthew Stout.

"It was proposed to me that I should help my downtrodden countrymen by assembling with other Irishmen to romance about 1798. Until Irishmen apply themselves to what the condition of Ireland will be in 1998 they will get very little patriotism out of Yours sincerely."

(George Bernard Shaw, 1898)

First published in 1998 by
Cork University Press,
National University of Ireland,
Cork, Ireland

© Kevin Whelan, 1998

All rights reserved. No part of this book may be reprinted or reproduced or utilised in any electronic, mechanical or other means, now known or hereafter invented, including photocopying and recording, or otherwise, without either the prior written permission of the Publishers or a license permitting restricted copying in Ireland issued by the Irish Copyright Licensing Agency Ltd, The Irish Writers' Centre, 19 Parnell Square, Dublin 1.

British Library Cataloguing in Publication Data
A CIP catalogue record for this book is available from the British Library.

ISBN 1 85918 210 0

Film Output by Phototypeset, Dublin
Printed by ColourBooks, Dublin

Contents

Foreword

The rebellion of 1798 was one of the most dramatic events in Irish history. The Bicentenary year of the rebellion has already been marked by many events throughout Ireland, under the auspices of the Government's 1798 Commemoration Committee. A major exhibition **Fellowship of Freedom. The United Irishmen and the Rebellion of 1798** by the National Library of Ireland and the National Museum of Ireland runs at the Museum's newly opened space at Collins Barracks in Dublin from May to December 1998.

Collaboration for the **Fellowship of Freedom** exhibition by the two institutions has been very successful. The rich documentary collections of the Library, including manuscripts, books, prints and drawings complement and add value to the artefacts held by the Museum, while the Museum's artefacts bring a real life three-dimensional aspect to the Library's documents. The location of the exhibition in Collins Barracks is highly suitable given the historical associations of the buildings with 1798.

We hope that this book by Professor Kevin Whelan, a companion volume to the Bicentenary Exhibition which he has helped to plan, will assist those who visit the exhibition, and other readers in gaining a better understanding of the background to the rebellion, the events of 1798 and the long-term consequences.

Brendan O'Donoghue
Director of the National Library of Ireland
Patrick F. Wallace
Director of the National Museum of Ireland

Now comes the night of carnage now the flesh of kings and princes
Pampered in palaces for our food the blood of captains nurturd
With lust and murder for our drink the drunken raven shall wander
All night among the slain and mock the wounded that groan in the field

(William Blake)

Preface

The 1790s were an extraordinary decade in Irish history, when the opportunity presented itself to transcend the age-old sectarian, ethnic and political divisions of the island. The United Irish movement had, as its central aim, the demolition of a political system rooted in sectarian privilege and its replacement with a secular democratic politics, founded on universal ideas of equality and justice. The project of creating a secular republic and recasting political participation on inclusive lines was deliberately blocked by the British state, using the weapons of sectarianism, military terror in 1798 and the suppression of the Irish parliament. We are still living with the consequences of those actions.

The 1790s are crucial in the evolution of modern Ireland. They gave birth to popular republicanism and loyalism, to separatism, to the Orange Order and Maynooth College; they generated peaks of optimism and pessimism, and finished in an insurrection which cost 30,000 lives (overwhelmingly on the popular side), more than were lost in the French Terror. The rebellion was followed by the Act of Union of 1800, which defined subsequent constitutional relationships between Ireland and Great Britain.

If the 1790s can be seen as the pivotal decade in the evolution of modern Ireland, then an honest and accurate understanding of these years is not just of scholarly interest, but has important implications for current political and cultural thinking. It is precisely because of its enduring relevance that 1798 has never truly passed out of politics and into history. The United Irishmen's ideas did not die with the events of 1798, but are still potent, valid and unrealised. In the sense that they faced the same problems which bedevil modern Ireland, the United Irishmen are very much our contemporaries.

Like the United Irishmen, we face the task today of negotiating an agreed political structure, capable of representing Irish people in all their inherited complexities. This volume stresses their enduring legacy – the political vision and moral choices which impelled men and women into the field in 1798. It is this political vision that this volume reclaims, not the physical defeat of the revolution on the bloody battlefields of '98. As Milan Kundera has noted, the struggle for power is the struggle of memory against forgetting. In the case of 1798, it is not what we remember that is the problem, but what we have forgotten.

As a seismic political event, the rebellion had a potent afterlife, which continued to affect Irish society for the following two centuries. The fluctuating interpretative trajectory of '98 after '98 is a reminder that the contest over meaning and value is a continuous one in any intellectually serious engagement with history.

While the past cannot be restored, memory can. This volume is motivated by a process of what the African-American novelist Toni Morrison describes as "rememoration" – a retrieving of memory which has been deliberately suppressed. Restoring this enabling memory can help release the circle of repetition: the endless calendrical cycle of Protestant memory or the mythic teleology of nationalist narrative can be redirected into historical and linear time, in which the possibility of progress again becomes available. By elevating politics out of the sectarian rut in which it has been deliberately confined since 1798, the dead weight of the past can be lifted and political buoyancy restored.

The United Irish project of an inclusive, democratic, non-sectarian Ireland remains uncompleted. By excavating its hidden meanings, 1798 becomes available in an entirely fresh way, opening an invigorating and generous space in which to consider the rebellion. As Walter Benjamin understood, to be forgotten is to die again: "Only the historian will have the gift of fanning the spark in the past who is firmly convinced that even the dead will not be safe from the enemy if he wins and this enemy has not ceased to be victorious."

This book approaches 1798 in the spirit of these remarks. It locates the rebellion in a generous chronological and geographical frame, freeing it from the spatial quarantine which reduces it to a set of cabbage-patch skirmishes, and the anxious fencing which seeks to corral the 1790s off from what preceded and followed it. The 1790s were in fact a hinge decade, which is equally crucial to an understanding of both the "long" eighteenth, and the "long" nineteenth centuries.

This volume values equally memory and history "proper". The power of political memory, which links past and present dynamically, needs to be a central interpretative focus in any understanding of 1798.

Unusually, this book is driven by the visual record of the rebellion and it bears the obvious traces of its origins in the Bicentenary Exhibition. Rather than mechanically using visual material as tangential illustrations to a textual treatment, the thematic and narrative framing is here supplied by the visual record itself. In this book the text is guided by the visual archive which illuminates historical and contemporary connections. This approach leads to a radically different perspective on the rebellion itself. To help the design structure of the project I have chosen to locate information relating to the illustrations in the appendix.

The 1790s have attracted significant new scholarship in the last two decades, spearheaded by senior scholars like L. M. Cullen, Marianne Elliott and Tom Bartlett. Their work in turn has inspired a revisiting of the canonical interpretations of the 1790s. The upsurge of fresh writing undertaken by many gifted historians has led to a thoroughgoing reinterpretation of the Rebellion, which is (broadly speaking) post-revisionist in its conclusions. Several publications by them are listed at the end of this book and insights made available by these scholars inform *Fellowship of Freedom*.

Kevin Whelan
Michael J. Smurfit Director of the
Dublin Centre of Irish Studies,
Notre Dame University.
Lá le Bríd, 1998

Acknowledgements

This book's genesis was as a companion volume to the major Bicentenary Exhibition on 1798 by the National Library of Ireland and National Museum of Ireland. I have been privileged to draw on the resources of these two great institutions, and this volume showcases their rich collections on the period. As a result, it has been possible to expand and redefine the narrow visual repertoire which has hitherto characterised writing on 1798.

Without the unstinting support of the staff of the National Library and National Museum this book would not have been possible. I would like to thank Brendan O'Donoghue (Acting Director), Catherine Fahy (Education Officer) and Collette O'Daly (Prints and Drawings) of the Library; Patrick Wallace (Director), Mairéad Dunleavy and Michael Kenny of the Museum. Eugene Hogan, National Library photographer was the key individual in generating the material for this book; his technical mastery of the new technologies in digital photography, his dedication to quality and his unwavering commitment are deeply appreciated. Lar Joye of the National Museum guided me through its collections with unrivalled authority and accuracy. Caroline Maloney, the exhibition designer, was also a tower of strength and support.

In physically producing this book, my greatest debt is to my friend and collaborator Matthew Stout. He designed the complex layout as well as supplying the cartography and burning the midnight oil. I am also grateful to my entirely supportive publishers, Cork University Press.

This book owes a great deal as always to friends and colleagues. I would like to thank Tom Bartlett, Marie Bourke, Bernard Browne, Brian Cleary, Peter Collins, Pat Cooke, Séamus Deane, Eamonn Doyle, Luke Gibbons, Tommy Graham, Tomás Hayes, Seamus Heaney, Mary Heffernan, Daire Keogh, Knight of Glin, Rolf Loeber, John McCabe, Perry McIntyre, Brendán MacSuibhne, Jenny Mayne, Máirín Ní Dhonnacadha, Willie Nolan, Éamonn Ó Ciardha, Stephen Rea, Helen Skrine and Eamonn Whelan. My final debt is to my family – Anne, Bébhinn, Fionn and Ruaidhrí – who live close to 1798 and who indulge a croppy boy.

THE TREE OF LIBERTY

Question: *What is that in your hand?*

Answer: *It is a branch.*

Question: *Of What?*

Answer: *Of the Tree of Liberty.*

Question: *Where did it first grow?*

Answer: *In America.*

Question: *Where does it bloom?*

Answer: *In France.*

Question: *Where did the seeds fall?*

Answer: *In Ireland.*

Question: *Where are you going to plant it?*

Answer: *In the Crown of Great Britain*

(United Irish Catechism, Cork, December 1797)

The American Revolution: Hope and History

"Life, liberty and the pursuit of happiness"

"The cause of America was the cause of Ireland. The cause of Ireland was the cause of America."

(Benjamin Franklin)

"We will not be their negroes."

(John Adams)

The Lambeg and Lisburn Volunteers Celebrating the Dungannon Convention

The Volunteers sprang into life in the spring of 1778. Faced with a possible French invasion threat and with a dilatory and negligent Dublin Castle response, Irish Protestants revamped the older militias, drawing on a long established Protestant self-defence reflex. From the start, the Volunteers were distanced from government and resolutely independent (refusing government pay, and electing their own officers). They acquired political dynamism as the independence campaign accelerated.

The American Revolution provided an enormous boost to Irish Radicalism. From the mid-eighteenth century onwards, both America and Ireland became aware of an intensifying British nationalism which treated Americans and Irish as colonial inferiors rather than as freeborn Britons. This galvanised the colonial élite in both countries into action. A typical response was to sharpen their self-identification as American or Irish.

Precisely because of this shared identity, the American Revolution impacted enormously on Ireland. The Volunteers, established as a citizen-army in 1778, were self-

"Nothing should be attempted that might bring about the possibility of a Union of civil interests between the Protestants and Papists of Ireland, whose antipathies and animosities all sound politicians will ever labour to keep alive."

(John Toland)

consciously Irish and resolutely distanced from government control. Overwhelmingly Protestant and middle-class, they quickly developed a national organisation as a paramilitary pressure group.

The Volunteers gave Irish "Patriot" opinion a focus and a forum. Astutely used by Henry Grattan, and facing a weak and divided English cabinet, the Volunteers authored the achievement of the "Constitution of 1782" and the establishment of "Grattan's Parliament". These patriots suggested that Ireland might follow the Americans in their search for independence.

PADDY'S RESOURCE

Paddy's Resource

Faced with English obstinacy, the Volunteers increasingly threatened violence. This cartoon shows "Paddy's Resource" in military terms. The cannon bears the ominous slogan "Free Trade or else", while the guns bear the ambiguous slogan "O Lord, open thou our lips and our mouths shall shew forth thy praise".

[MAP]

Presbyterians as a percentage of total population, 1834

- 0
- 5
- 20
- 50

Derry, Donegal, Derry, Antrim, Donegal, Tyrone, Belfast, Enniskillen, Fermanagh, Armagh, Down, Monaghan, Newry, Cavan

N

0   30 km

"A sudden light from America shone through our prison."
(Dublin Society of United Irishmen, 1796)

Charlemont, leader of the Ulster Volunteers

Ulster Presbyterians

The heartland of Volunteering was east Ulster where the Volunteers spread like wildfire in the Presbyterian districts. Belfast was the Volunteer capital, more politically radical and less gentry-led in its politics than Dublin. The Ulster Presbyterians, with close links to America, followed the American War carefully and were especially heartened by the separation of Church and State in the American constitution – a notable victory for Presbyterianism.

George Washington

George Washington quickly became the icon of the emerging American Republic, the modern incarnation of the classical citizen–soldier–statesman. Ireland and America shared a common political language of liberty, corruption, rights and civic virtue. From the mid-eighteenth century onwards, they also shared a sharpening awareness of a more exclusionary trend within an intensifying British nationalism (metropolitan, militant, Protestant) and an expanding empire. Britishness defined itself in an exclusive rather than inclusive way. The shock of rejection as colonial inferiors rather than as freeborn Britons humiliated and haunted the colonial élite in both Ireland and America. Their self-identification as Irish or American emerged from a hurt reaction to this British projection of difference. In both Ireland and America, Washington symbolised this refusal of second-class status as perennially juvenile partners in empire. In 1783, the great man rejoiced in Ireland's political progress "I would felicitate the Kingdom of Ireland on their emancipation from British controul".

British Museum

"America is the paradise of the poor man, who was accustomed to a labouring life; in Europe, his toil is unable to afford him one wholesome meal in the year; in America, it furnishes him with one every day. If political attachments draws him to America, he finds the cheapest and free'st government in the world — the equality so much ridiculed in Europe, as visionary theory, is no longer mere speculation in the western republic."

(Watty Cox)

Royal Society of Arts, London

James Barry (Self-Portrait)

The Phoenix or the Resurrection of Freedom by James Barry

This engraving captures a dominant sentiment that the English tradition of liberty had been extinguished by the corrupt conduct of the American war. Liberty had migrated across the Atlantic to be reborn in its American mode. James Barry, a committed republican, draws attention to the celebrated earlier incarnations of republicanism in Athens, Rome and Florence, and the death of its English version due to a corrupt aristocratic and monarchical interest. Liberty has taken "flight to a new people of manners simple and untainted". The bier of a prostrate English liberty is surrounded by a grieving pantheon of Whig heroes – Milton, Sidney, Marvell, Locke (and Barry himself!) – who wave in valediction to the American shore, where the Republican Phoenix rises from a classical temple, set amidst a utopian landscape of arcadian simplicity.

N.M.I.

James Napper Tandy

George Washington

Tandy, a gregarious, rambunctious ironmonger, emerged as popular successor to Charles Lucas as the idol of the radical Dublin middle class, supported by the guilds, the merchants and the artisans. This print deliberately echoes American treatments of Washington. Tandy, in Volunteer uniform, holds in his hand a scroll drawing attention to his proposed political "Congress", at which the radical issues of parliamentary reform and Catholic Emancipation would be discussed.

SUD AN NIDH GHUIDHIMSI SAXONIG

Asig [aiseag] is sguilluicht [scaoileacht] bioch sin eatturtha
crith is bóthán fuar is morchuid deatuig ann
broan anuas ó Luan go Sathuran suisin cruaidh air spruain beg easarach
maoila dearaga is dreancudh do bhfearfuin bualladh buaint is grafadh doibh
reabadh branir is doith an aoil

tothchuilt na dioghe buighe go eadurtha
rómhar na claisidhe is deanamh cloide
sgadán caoch mar bheile taniomhthach

bócuna [bocanna] beana is graine alluin reo [leo]
cead [céad] ri ra ar sgalladh praisge theith
do thocfuich manamna mor na ccriodha
anngur cleibh ar an te bhearfach a thuille doibh

HERE ARE THE THINGS THAT I WISH·FOR THE SAXONS

Vomiting and Diarrhoea, Shivers and Shakes and Heartaches
A Cold Cabin Blinded With Smoke
The Rain Dripping Down on Them From Monday to Saturday
A Hard Floor, As a Bed, With a Scatter of Straw
Fleas and Lice Constantly at Them.

Thrashing, Binding, and Hoeing
Turning the Sod and Burning the Lime
Digging the Drains and Making Ditches.

Their Best Meal White Bucks [bad potatoes]
With No Dip Only a Grain of Salt
Scalding Porridge That Will Give Them Indigestion
And May Anyone That Gives Them More Get a Heart Attack

Burns Library, Boston College

Cormac Common, fin-Szealaizhe. Ætatis sua 89

Colmán Mac Carthaigh's poem on the American Revolution

Although the painfully cautious Catholic leadership ostentatiously paraded their loyalty throughout the American War, the poorer Catholics thought differently: "the lower class are to a man attached to the Americans". Colmán Mac Carthaigh's poem on the American Revolution and the Volunteers begins with a measured political commentary on the progress of the war and its Irish implications. However, its conclusion abruptly shifts register, reverting to conventional Jacobite mode, with a searing, bitter, racial onslaught on the English in Ireland. This volatile mix of modern and archaic, of closely observed socio-economic detail and broad cultural generalisation of politics and history was characteristic of both the Whiteboy and the later Defender secret societies.

> *"Presbyterians went in thousands to America and if ships had been found, thousands more would have sought a peaceful asylum in that land of liberty – a happy refuge from the despotism of England."*

(Rev. William Campbell, Moderator of the Presbyterian Synod)

> *"Every citizen here is in his own country. To the Protestant, it is a Protestant country; to the Catholic, a Catholic country and the Jew, if he pleases, may establish in it his own New Jerusalem."*

(William Sampson)

Certificate of the Hibernian Society of Philadelphia

This shows America welcoming Irish immigrants. The successful American experiment added a new vocabulary and a new reference to the language of liberty. The Strabane-born printer of the American Declaration of Independence, John Dunlop, reported from Philadelphia in 1785: "The young men of Ireland who wish to be free and happy should leave it and come here as quick as possible. There is no place in the world where a man meets so rich a reward for good conduct and industry as in America."

Winterthur Museum

The Irish Volunteers by Francis Wheatley (detail)

This dramatic canvas represents an entirely new genre of history painting, willing to locate a specific event in an actual location and dispensing with stylised classical motifs, exotic locations, and elaborate allegory. The painting, first exhibited in May 1780, is entirely contemporary, depicting the celebrated Volunteer gathering in Dublin on 4 November 1779, an impressive orchestration and display of the Irish body politic, the citizen soldiers of an emerging Irish nation. Key figures are instantly recognisable – James Napper Tandy, the Duke of Leinster, John Fitzgibbon, Luke Gardiner, the Earl of Charlemont. The focus is the equestrian statue of William of Orange, Protestant icon of the Whig tradition and emblem of civil liberties. At the demonstration, the cannon bore the pointed slogan "Free Trade or this". "Free Trade" signified the removal of vexatious restrictions on Irish exports and imports to and from the British colonies. (The American crisis deepened a war-time depression.) English trade restrictions could then be presented as a classic example of the cavalier way in which Ireland's commercial interests were handled, due to Ireland's constitutional subordination. This potent fusion of commercial and constitutional grievance fuelled the political campaign of the Volunteers.

N.G.I.

Huntington Library

America. A Prophesy by William Blake

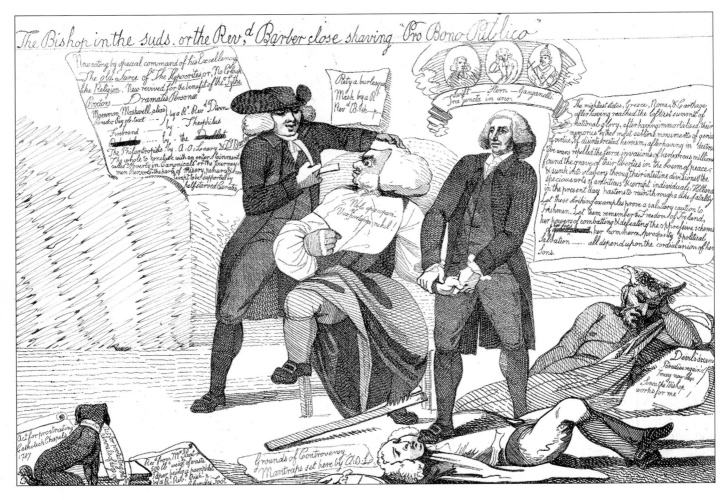

The Bishop in the Suds

This cartoon refers to the celebrated paper war of the late 1780s, in which the concept of "Protestant Ascendancy" began to solidify. Its main protagonist was Bishop Charles Agar, shown here as "The Bishop in the Suds" who is being shaved by Dr Samuel Barber, who opposed him from the Presbyterian perspective, and by Rev. Arthur O'Leary, who presented the Catholic position.

Dates of Birth, United Irishmen

1760	Oliver Bond, William Tennent, Rev. James Porter	1765	Robert Holmes
1761	Edward Hay, Samuel Neilson, Robert Simms	1766	Peter Finnerty, William Orr, John Sheares
1762	Bagenal Harvey, Roger O'Connor, Rev. James Coigly	1767	Henry Joy McCracken, Thomas Russell, William Orr
1763	W. J. MacNevin, William Simms, Arthur O'Connor Edward Fitzgerald, Theobald Wolfe Tone	1768	Henry Monro
		1769	John Henry Colclough
1764	William Sampson, Thomas Addis Emmet, James Hope	1770	Edward Fitzgerald (Newpark)

Henry Grattan

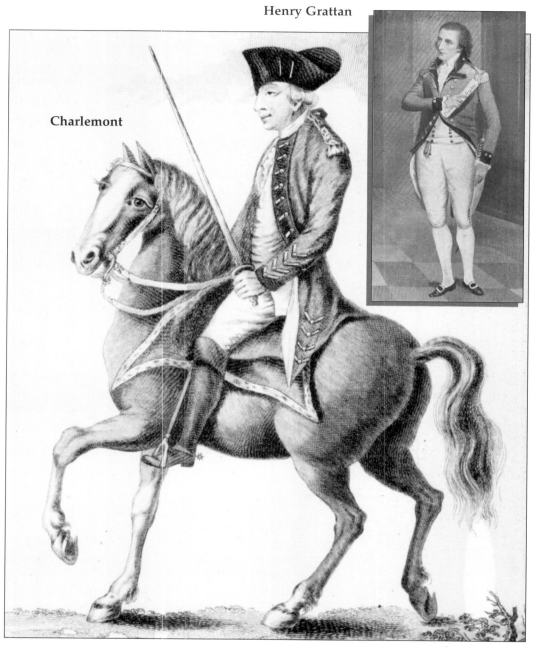

Charlemont

"I regretted not being an American; I made up my mind that if I ever could, I would play the same role in Ireland."

(Archibald Hamilton Rowan on the American Revolution)

The American Revolution provided an enormous boost to Irish radicalism. As Henry Flood expressed it: "A voice from America had shouted to liberty, the echo of it caught your people as it passed along the Atlantic and they re-echoed the voice till it reverberated here." Most of the influential leaders of the United Irishmen were born in the 1760s and were literally as well as politically children of the American Revolution. The key question for the Irish Volunteer Movement was whether it would follow the American example, as with Grattan, or meekly retreat into its colonial shell, as with Charlemont.

Britishness and Irishness: The Other Within

"Beef and Liberty"

**The Gates of Calais or the Roast Beef of Old England
by William Hogarth, 1748.**

In print form, this became a staple of anti-French propaganda for generations. A waiter carries an enormous roast beef towards the English Inn in Calais. He is surveyed by a salivating fat friar, a disconsolate Scottish fugitive (complete with bagpipes) from the abortive 1745 Jacobite invasion, and a scrawny Irish "Wild Goose" (who spills his thin French soup at the sight of the succulent beef). In the background, the French kneel before the host in a public display of superstition. Meanwhile, the sunlight falls on the royal arms of England, emblazoned on the gates of Calais, a symbol of the former English presence in France. Beef represented the free-born Englishman, as opposed to the frivolous French. Roast beef became the symbol of the strong constitution of England, the political muscle of John Bull. The popularity of Hogarth's print indicated the extent to which Britishness was projected against a French backdrop, Catholic and despotic in character. (Tate Gallery, London)

The Volunteers authored the achievement of the "Constitution of 1782" and the establishment of "Grattan's Parliament". They believed that Ireland might follow the Americans in their search for independence. However, the much vaunted settlement of 1782 turned out to be a hollow victory. Without reform, which raised the vexed and divisive issue of Catholic rights, the Irish parliament remained vulnerable to a controlling English interest. Parliamentary reformers agonised over "Catholic emancipation". The necessary reform could only be achieved by admitting Catholics and it was a fundamental principle of the English Whig version of liberty that Catholics were incapable of exercising democratic responsibilities. The imposition of penal laws and the establishment of a sectarian state was inevitable. So was the maintenance of a three-tier society, with the Anglicans as first-class, the Presbyterians as second-class and the Catholic majority as third-class members.

Despite its enormous later reputation, "Grattan's Parliament" quickly proved a major disappointment. Having traumatically lost its American colonies, Britain gave more sustained attention to the anomalous situation of Ireland – no longer one of fourteen Atlantic colonies, but now its only colony in that area. Precisely because it had potentially greater power, "Grattan's Parliament" was more tightly controlled than ever before.

The Volunteer movement proved incapable of maintaining its radical momentum, because it split acrimoniously on the issue of admitting Catholics to citizenship. This in turn paralysed the parliamentary reform movement.

The great optimism released by the achievement of the "Constitution of 1782" subsided into a sullen sectarian stalemate by the end of the decade. The settlement had increased rather than decreased Irish–English tensions: the sectarian temperature was rising and the countryside was once more convulsed by secret societies. Irish radicalism seemed hopelessly trapped in a sectarian cul-de-sac.

Leeds City Art Gallery

Grattan's Parliament

In the nineteenth century, when the Home Rule issue dominated politics, the independent Irish parliament of the late-eighteenth century acquired an enormous symbolic value, summarised in the resonant mantra "Grattan's Parliament". Despite the theatrical set pieces and rhetorical rockets of Grattan and Curran, and its subsequent romanticisation, the 1780s parliament was tightly controlled. Having lost its Atlantic colonies, Britain gave Ireland more serious attention. English strategists were worried about the unworkability and volatility of the new relationship. Unable to push through their preference for a Union, they sought throughout the 1780s to assert control by cultivating a new group of political handlers – notably John Foster, John Fitzgibbon and John Beresford. "The Three Jacks" were all ambitious, skillful politicians, resolutely anglophile. All were new men, outside the traditionally powerful networks of Irish politics. They became the crucial managers of the Irish parliament. For the radicals, these men were the epitome of Irish corruption, who cynically served the English interest in Ireland to enhance their own careers.

The Three Jacks or the Hunt of Erin

This shows Ireland as a defenceless female (carrying the uncrowned harp, symbol of the United Irishmen), viciously pursued by the three-headed hound, an allusion to Foster, Fitzgibbon and Beresford. This cartoon appeared in the *Irish Magazine* of Watty Cox, inveterate populist scourge of Ascendancy Ireland.

The Louth Mower (detail)

Foster sent the military to break up a pattern at Tallanstown in County Louth.

John Fitzgibbon as Lord Chancellor

Fitzgibbon became the first eighteenth-century Irishman to be elevated to the highest legal post in Ireland. He is here depicted by the fashionable American painter, Gilbert Stuart, in his robes of office. Fitzgibbon had a *nouveau-riche* streak, indulged in his love of display, most ostentatiously obvious in the flashy new carriage he imported from England in 1790. Despite (or because?) he was the son of a convert, "Black Jack" was notoriously opposed to Catholic claims to political power.

John Foster as Speaker

"The Louth Mower"

John Foster's grandfather had allegedly been a common farmer but Foster now owned a vast estate at Collon in County Louth. He was a capable politician, who supported Protestant Ascendancy and tough law-and-order measures, including the full use of military force to suppress popular agitation.

R.I.A.

The Custom House
Non-Pareil

John Beresford, at the height of his power, was known as "The King of Ireland", through his control of patronage in the revenue system. Installed in palatial quarters at the Custom House (his pet project, built in the teeth of bitter popular and mercantile opposition), Beresford was seen as a corrupt politician, involved in shady property speculation (notably in the vicinity of the Custom House).

Les Régiments de Bulkeley, de Roscommon, de Dillon, de Berwick et de Clare (Irlandais) en 1770

Mellon Foundation

The "Wild Geese": Irish regiments in the service of France, 1770

Given their seventeenth-century scattering and their subservient political position at home, Irish Catholics quickly constructed a diasporic dimension. By the mid-eighteenth century, three key elements in the Irish Catholic nation existed overseas – intellectual (the Irish colleges), military (the Irish Brigade) and commercial (in the mercantile network that rimmed Atlantic Europe). Due to their widespread connections, Irish Catholics were well aware of their degraded conditions at home. Throughout the century, the "Wild Geese" of the Irish Brigades remained a constant focus of Catholic hopes and Protestant fears – especially at moments of political tension or evolution.

Richard Hennessy

Charles Carroll

Student at Salamanca

Two good examples of Catholic success abroad were Richard Hennessy and Charles Carroll. Hennessy, from the Blackwater Valley in Cork, joined the Wild Geese, and later settled in Cognac where he pioneered the production of brandy. Carroll, from a family displaced from their old base at Birr Castle in the Ely O'Carroll territory, had risen to prominence at Carrollton in Maryland, eventually becoming the only Catholic signatory of the American Declaration of Independence. He was painted by Joshua Reynolds, a tribute to his wealth and fame. Throughout his long life, Carroll never forgot his Offaly origins, or the prestige once enjoyed by his family.

Pinacoteca Nazionale, Bologna

Philoctetes on the Island of Lemnos
by James Barry

Barry paints a national allegory of the Catholic body politic, a visual equivalent of the Munster Aisling tradition. Philoctetes had been banished to the island because his fellow citizens could not tolerate the offensive stench from his unstaunched leg wound. In Barry's highly theatrical version, the focus is on the open wound (of colonialism?), barely concealed by inadequate bandages. An emotional Philoctetes – degraded, enslaved, islanded, deprived of his patrimony, "a foreigner in his native land" – draws explicit attention to his wound. Instead of the evasive Catholic leadership stance of ostentatious loyalty, Barry urges them to tackle the painful reality of their situation – "to weep and bare it" instead of "to grin and bear it". From the 1780s onwards, this more assertive stance appealed to a younger generation of Catholic activists.

Crawford Gallery, Cork

Ulysses and Polyphemus by James Barry

Edmund Burke in the guise of Ulysses and Barry as his companion, flee from Polyphemus, the one-eyed Cyclops. The worldly-wise and prudent Burke cautions Barry to prudent discretion ("silence, exile and cunning") as they escape the Cyclops – a version of the blind bigotry and indiscriminate violence of Irish Protestant Ascendancy.

Edmund Burke

Rooted firmly in the Catholic culture of Munster, educated in a Cork hedge school, and with Catholic relations in the Blackwater Valley, Burke became the most persuasive spokesman for Catholic claims to full inclusion in the British state and empire. Burke's "great melody" (Yeats), linking the Penal Laws to similar imperial excesses in America and India, envisaged an empire which could endorse diversity of culture. With this in mind, he sought to accommodate Catholic Ireland within Protestant Britain.

15

Old Burras Chapel, 1776

The Catholic Church endured a difficult situation in the eighteenth century. By law non-existent, it retained the allegiance of over three-quarters of the population, and developed an intimate, domestic and vernacular spiritual life, far divorced from the pomp and power of institutional continental Catholicism. This depiction of the chapel near Castletown in County Laois captures the dilapidation which characterised the public face of Irish Catholicism in the eighteenth century.

"Ninety years ago the question was, whether Popery and arbitrary power should be established in the person of King James, or freedom and the Protestant religion in the person of King William – four-fifths of the inhabitants of Ireland adhered to the cause of King James; they were defeated, and I rejoice in their defeat. The laws that followed this event were not laws of persecution, but of political necessity."

(Henry Flood)

Hedge School

This hedge school at Ballycoris on the Mullet peninsula in County Mayo was photographed by the anthropologist C. R. Browne *c.*1890. Faced with the legal banning of Catholic education, the Catholic community had constructed a remarkably efficient informal education system, one effect of which was to rapidly increase the anglophone component of the population, especially in the south-eastern quadrant of the island. The spread of literacy in English was an important precondition for the mass politicisation of the 1790s. The term "hedge" in contemporary usage referred to untrained or unqualified practitioners – as in hedge-lawyer, hedge-carpenter, hedge-doctor, etc. It did not refer to the literal fact of classes being held in the open air.

The Irish House of Parliament by Edward Pearse

Although they constituted the overwhelming majority of the Irish population, Catholics were forbidden by law to be members of parliament.

"The Irish Protestant will never be free while the Catholic is a slave." (Henry Grattan)

The Harvest Dance at Rosanna
by Maria Spilsbury

This charming painting depicts a strawboy performance in front of the great window of the Tighe mansion near Ashford in County Wicklow. It celebrates a patriarchal, paternalist relationship between landlord and tenant, into which no threatening political menace intrudes. In the 1790s, such idyllic images, evoking a nostalgic elegy for a lost landlord world of harmonious social relations, disappeared.

Private Collection

The Right Boys Paying Their Tythes, 1785-1786

The issue of tithes — a tax paid to the established Anglican church by all religious denominations — vexed Catholics and Presbyterians throughout the eighteenth century, and was especially onerous for the rural poor. The agrarian secret societies — the Whiteboys and Rightboys of Munster — used intimidatory violence against tithe proctors as a warning against excessive demands. This hostile caricature shows them whipping one naked victim, burying another up to his neck in a furze-lined pit, and burning the ricks of another. The image of a riotous, violent mob increasingly haunted conservative imaginings in the late eighteenth century.

17

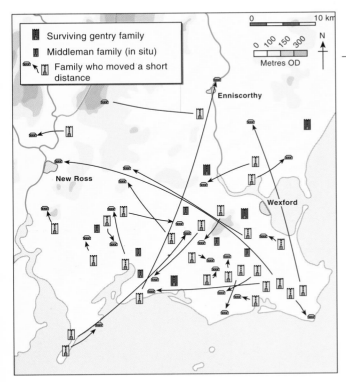

Dispersal of South Wexford Families, 1650-1730

The seventeenth-century confiscations uprooted the existing Catholic gentry. Rather than going "to Hell or to Connaught", most settled locally as middlemen and farmers, retaining their position as the political and cultural leaders of their communities, and exercising greater influence than the new landlord class. A gentry of the blood rather than of the sword, these families saw themselves, and were seen as an underground gentry, unjustly displaced by an iniquitous régime. Here flourished the Hidden Ireland of the eighteenth century, which sustained the Jacobite language of redemption and restoration. Land ownership remained a live political issue in Irish society throughout the eighteenth century. The publication of Charles O'Conor's map of the ancestral locations of Irish families touched a raw colonial nerve and caused a furore. O'Conor was accused of seeking to overturn the seventeenth-century settlement, fomenting the Catholic masses to reinstate the ancient proprietors. As a tiny minority, the Anglican landed élite felt threatened by any efforts to deepen the knowledge of Irish pre-colonial history.

The Underground Gentry

Rathronan House, the Brown Family Home

The Browns could trace their continuous occupation back to 1170, and they regained possession as tenants in the early eighteenth century. Their newly built farmhouse adjoined their ancestral castle – material testimony to the durability of this underground gentry.

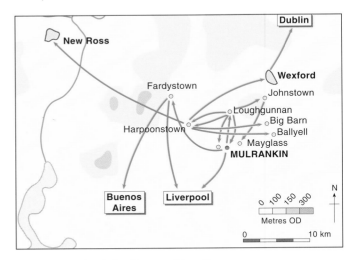

The Spread of the Brown Family

If these families are traced through time, it quickly becomes clear that a widening circle of Catholic families in the eighteenth century could legitimately claim to be descended from dispossessed gentry. Such families tended to intermarry and in the prosperous Catholic areas of Munster and Leinster; the big-farm class was largely derived from this group.

> *"Elsewhere landed title was purchase, in Ireland it was forfeiture. The old proprietor kept alive the memory of his claim. Property in Ireland resembled the thin soil of volcanic countries spread lightly over subterranean fires."*
>
> (Arthur Browne, 1787)

The Brown Family Tree

These family dynasties were also intensely rooted. In the case of the Browns, the closely-woven web of family interests remained firmly constellated around the Mulrankin base.

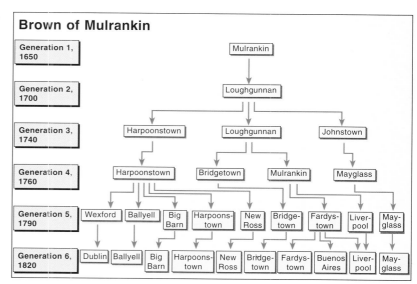

Brown of Mulrankin

GOING TO MASS

ITS BOTHERATION LUCKY that I put on my SUNDAY SHOES or by SAINT PATRICK I should have got my feet wet.

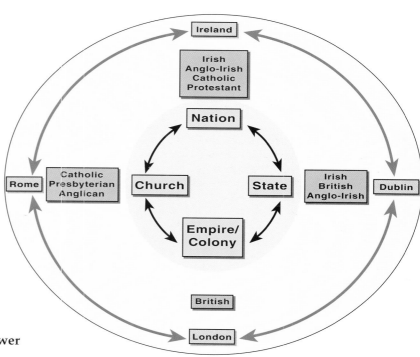

The Matrix of Power

By the late eighteenth century, the Irish problem had assumed complex proportions. How could one reconcile the conflicting traditions and political demands of Irish, English and Scottish, or Catholic, Protestant and Dissenter? How could the claims of empire be balanced against those of church, state and nation? How were the desires of the nation and the power of the state to be reconciled? The matrix of power was fundamentally volatile, liable to become unstable under the pressure of political change. The situation lent itself to zero-sum analyses, in which gains for one side were seen as losses for the other. The task of constructing a viable political arrangement which could convincingly claim to represent these varying stances was an endlessly complex one.

The Impact of the French Revolution: "The Morning Star of Liberty"

"Liberté, egalité, fraternité"

"To subvert the tyranny of our execrable government, to break the connection with England, the never-failing cause of all our political evil, and to assert the independence of my country — these were my objects. To unite the whole people of Ireland, to abolish the memory of all past dissensions, and to substitute the common name of Irishmen in place of the denominations of Protestants, Catholics and Dissenters — these were my means."

(Theobald Wolfe Tone)

"Our Gallic brethren were born July 14th 1789. Alas, we are still in embryo."

(United Irish toast, 1792)

The Conquerors of the Bastille by Hippolyte Delaroche

(Musée Carnavalet, Paris)

The French Revolution freed the gridlock in Irish politics. By breaking the sectarian mould of European politics, the French Revolution answered the intransigent sectarian questions: Catholics could now be safely admitted as citizens, ensuring that the Penal Laws and the maintenance of a sectarian state was no longer necessary. The Irish three-tier society of Anglicans, Presbyterians and Catholics could now be reconstituted as a single community of United Irishmen.

Theobald Wolfe Tone, William Drennan, Samuel Neilson and Thomas Russell proposed the creation of the United Irishmen with a political project of common citizenship and parity of esteem for the main traditions of Ireland. Fired by French ideals in the heady days of the 1790s when it seemed that all Europe would be swept by the new republican politics, the United Irishmen were established in a blaze of optimism in Belfast and Dublin in 1791.

The French Revolution made buoyant the weight of history – the dead hand of the dead generations, weighing like a nightmare on the brains of the living. The Revolution's promotion of human rights offered an alternative path to the idea of a political community. The universality of the Republican principles provided a neutral language with which to consider the characteristics of a just state.

There were three novel elements in the United Irish programme. The first was its ability to transcend the overwhelming anti-popery of the existing Whig tradition. A second was a fully-fledged separatism, symbolised by the uncrowned harp. Unlike the integrationist and unionist dynamic of the Scottish enlightenment, the United Irishmen embraced separatism as a necessary prelude to parliamentary reform. Any English connection acted as a prop for the junta which ran the country on English lines, for their own interest. The third element was an effort to grant equal worth to Irish culture, by lengthening the time-line of Irish history to include its pre-colonial past.

The Fall of the Bastille

SONGS ON THE
FRENCH REVOLUTION.
That took place at Paris, 14th July, 1789:
Sung at the *Celebration* thereof at BELFAST on
Saturday, 14th July, 1792.

TO WHICH ARE ADDED
FOUR OTHER SONGS.

BELFAST : Printed in the year 1792.

"The French Revolution had roused Irishmen from a sleep of centuries. They indeed awoke but to a sense of their misery and a sight of their chains."

(Bernard Dornin)

Bastille Day, Belfast, 1793

The impact of the French Revolution on Ireland was to release the sectarian stalemate. The leading Catholic power in Europe had, astonishingly, produced a revolution more radical than the much vaunted Glorious (and Protestant) Revolution of 1688. The reception of the French Revolution in Ireland was as a Catholic effort at liberty. This was especially important to the Presbyterians, steeped in the Bible and the Book of Revelations, who were inclined to see the Revolution as a millennial event, signifying the long-awaited destruction of popery. The fall of the Bastille quickly became the accepted symbol of the Revolution, and the occasion was enthusiastically celebrated in Belfast in the early 1790s. The emphasis on 14 July also conveniently underplayed the divisive 12 July celebrations, as the Williamite tradition increasingly became conservative and staunchly Protestant. For Irish radicals, the French Revolution suggested that hope and history might now indeed rhyme in an Irish context.

The Edgeworth Family by Adam Buck

An enlightened group was emerging within the Irish Anglican élite, represented politically by Henry Grattan, the Fitzgeralds and other Irish Whigs. The Edgeworth family of Edgeworthstown in County Longford were a good example. Richard Lovell Edgeworth (1744-1817) was a classic *philosophe* – improving landlord, experimental scientist, inventor, pedagogue and political theorist. His daughter Maria (1767-1847) was to become an important Irish novelist. Within such circles, enlightened ideas spread, in which responsible Protestant landlords would lead their Catholic tenants towards improved social values, and incorporate them

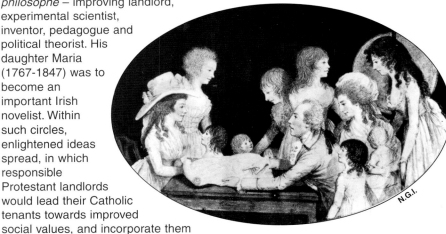

safely into British society. Edgeworth's celebrated novel *Castle Rackrent* was a whig attack on the feckless irresponsibility of the Irish landed class. This charming group portrait by Adam Buck was painted in 1784. Richard is shown with his young family and new wife, discussing a drawing of one of his inventions with Maria, his eldest and favourite daughter, shown seated at extreme left. The Cork-born Adam Buck was later to be identified as an United Irishman by a London spy.

"That nation [France] renowned in arts and arms will now be the refuge and asylum of the brave and good in every nation. Seated in the midst of Europe like a lily on a hill to shed Light, Liberty and Humanity all around. Happy Country! where the Rights of Man are sacred, no Bastille to imprison the body, nor religious establishment to shackle the soul."

(Rev. Samuel Barber, Moderator of the General Synod, 1791)

Rainbow Coalition

The Society of United Irishmen was a rainbow coalition which successfully fused hitherto divergent traditions in Irish politics. The Dublin United Irishmen, for example, were split equally between Catholic and Protestant, and were drawn from the Guilds, the Whigs, the Catholic Committee and the Volunteers.

Theobald Wolfe Tone

Tone became the main interpreter of the French Revolution for an Irish audience with his enormously successful pamphlet *Argument on behalf of the Catholics of Ireland*. Tone argued that the old equation between Catholicism and despotism had been rendered obsolete by the Revolution and that Irish Catholics would demonstrate the same political maturity as their French counterparts. Once Catholics could be accepted as citizens, the parliamentary reform movement could at last achieve its aims. It was in this sense that Tone described the Revolution as "the morning star of liberty" in Ireland. Tone's pamphlet broke the sectarian mould of Irish politics. With Russell, Neilson and Drennan, he proposed the creation of the United Irishmen with a political project of common citizenship and equal esteem for the main traditions of Ireland.

Theobald Wolfe Tone

Samuel Neilson

Thomas Russell

William Drennan

Oliver Bond

James Hope

Archibald Hamilton Rowan

Richard Dry

Brotherhood of Affection

"May God eternally damn the soul of the man who subscribes the first guinea."

(Thomas McCabe on a proposal to establish a slaving company in Belfast)

"On every lump of sugar, I see a drop of human blood."

(Thomas Russell)

Wedgewood Anti-Slavery Plate

United Irish writing was suffused with the rhetoric of slavery and emancipation. They made an explicit connection between political degradation in Ireland and the condition of slaves in America.

Key United Irishmen

Theobald Wolfe Tone   From a minor Anglican family in County Kildare, Tone had been educated at Trinity College Dublin and trained to be a lawyer. Brilliant, affable but restless, his political energies received their first concentration in the United Irish movement, of which he was the main architect. Tone coined their name, and personally bridged the enormous chasm between Catholic activists, the parliamentary reform movement and the radical Ulster Presbyterians.

Samuel Neilson   Son of a Presbyterian clergyman, and prosperous young merchant, Neilson was the driving organisational energy behind the Belfast Society of United Irishmen. He was also the very effective editor of their newspaper the *Northern Star*.

Thomas Russell   Cork-born Anglican and former army officer in India, Thomas Russell was a bosom friend of Tone's and a central figure in the birth of the United Irish movement. Sociable, intelligent, handsome, he and Tone were the bridge builders between the northern Presbyterians and the southern radicals and Catholics. As such, he was a crucial catalyst in the United Irishmen's rainbow coalition.

William Drennan   Scion of one of the most intellectual and influential of Ulster Presbyterian families, Drennan was a consummate phrase-maker and prose stylist. He was the principal author of the early publications of the United Irishmen.

Oliver Bond   Son of a Donegal clergyman, he was a highly respected and successful woollen merchant in Dublin. As a leading United Irishman, his Ulster connections ensured that he became a key linkman between the southern and northern organisation.

James Hope   The son of a Scottish immigrant of stern Covenanting stock, he was a self-taught weaver from the intensely radical and Presbyterian Templepatrick area of east Antrim. Unflinchingly committed to the poor whom he saw as the real victims of Ireland's iniquitous political structure, Hope was a pioneer socialist.

Archibald Hamilton Rowan   Born at Killyleagh Castle in County Down, he later purchased an estate at Rathcoffey in County Kildare. As a prominent landowner, Volunteer and Whig, he was a glittering prize for the United Irishmen when he agreed to become secretary to the Dublin Society.

Richard Dry   Born into a Wexford Protestant family, Dry became active in Dublin politics, including the Guilds, the Defenders and the United Irishmen. A gifted popular organiser, he was eventually arrested and transported to Botany Bay. His son was later to become Prime Minister of Tasmania.

Linen Hall Library

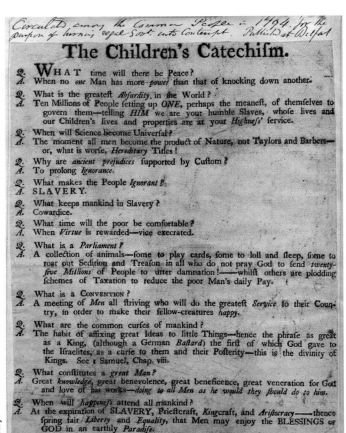

The Children's Catechism.

Circulated among the Common People ℔ 1794 for the purpose of turning regal sort into contempt. Publish'd at Belfast

Q. **WHAT** time will there be Peace?
A. When no *one* Man has more power than that of knocking down another.

Q. What is the greatest *Absurdity*, in the World?
A. Ten Millions of People setting up ONE, perhaps the meaneſt, of themselves to govern them—telling HIM we are your humble Slaves, whoſe lives and our Children's lives and properties are at your *Highneſs'* service.

Q. When will Science become Univerſal?
A. The moment all men become the product of Nature, not Taylors and Barbers—or, what is worſe, *Hereditary* Titles!

Q. Why are *ancient prejudices* ſupported by Cuſtom?
A. To prolong *Ignorance*.

Q. What makes the People Ignorant?
A. SLAVERY.

Q. What keeps mankind in Slavery?
A. Cowardice.

Q. What time will the poor be comfortable?
A. When *Virtue* is rewarded—vice execrated.

Q. What is a *Parliament*?
A. A collection of animals—ſome to play cards, ſome to loll and ſleep, ſome to roar out Sedition and Treaſon in all who do not pray God to ſend *twenty-five Millions* of People to utter damnation!——whilſt others are plodding ſchemes of Taxation to reduce the poor Man's daily Pay.

Q. What is a *Convention*?
A. A meeting of *Men* all ſtriving who will do the greateſt *Service* to their Country, in order to make their fellow-creatures *happy*.

Q. What are the common curſes of mankind?
A. The habit of affixing great Ideas to little Things—hence the phraſe as great as a King, (although a German *Baſtard*) the firſt of which God gave to the Iſraelites, as a curſe to them and their Poſterity—this is the divinity of Kings. See 1 Samuel, Chap. viii.

Q. What conſtitutes a *great Man*?
A. Great *knowledge*, great *benevolence*, great *beneficence*, great *veneration* for God and love of his works—*doing to all Men as he would they ſhould do to him.*

Q. When will *happineſs* attend all mankind?
A. At the expiration of SLAVERY, Prieſtcraft, *Kingcraft*, and *Ariſtocracy*——thence ſpring fair *Liberty* and *Equality*, that Men may enjoy the BLESSINGS of GOD in an earthly *Paradiſe*.

N. B. The friends of Humanity will, undoubtedly, *teach* their Children this Catechiſm.

Ha! ha! ha! GOD SAVE the *KING!!* *Ha! ha! ba!!*

Children's Catechism

This piece of propaganda is aimed at a juvenile audience.

A National Volunteer, 1792

Fired by French ideals during the heady days of the early 1790s when it seemed that Enlightenment principles would receive universal political expression, the United Irishmen were established in a blaze of optimism in Belfast and Dublin in 1791. From the beginning, they were a self-consciously national organisation but their core strength initially was in Presbyterian east Ulster.

Northern Star Sales Network

The United Irishmen were skilled propagandists, with many printers, writers and editors attracted to their cause. Their newspaper, the *Northern Star*, established in 1791, was innovative in being the first to be run by a board of directors. It was also beautifully printed and contained a large proportion of Irish news. Brilliantly edited by Samuel Neilson, it reached the limits of contemporary technology at 4,200 copies. The *Star* was most popular in the Presbyterian heartland of east Ulster, especially in south-east Antrim, north Down, and east Tyrone. Its rival, the more conservative *Belfast Newsletter*, circulated mainly in Anglican areas, especially in north Armagh. The success of the *Star* as the paper of the "turbulent opulent" greatly disturbed government. A loyalist reported in 1797: "A set of young merchants in Belfast set up a newspaper called the *Northern Star*, not with a view to gain but almost avowedly for revolutionary purposes. It was ably conducted and its success decisive, the country being completely corrupted or dangerously infected so far as the delivery of the *Northern Star* extends and no farther." The government responded by subsidising the *Newsletter* (until 1829) and by militarily smashing the *Star* in May 1797.

Book Clubs in Ulster

1.	Doagh (Antrim)	1770
2.	Belfast (Antrim)	1781
3.	Portaferry (Down)	1786
4.	Newry (Down)	1786
5.	Newtownards (Down)	1789
6.	Lowtown (Antrim)	1790
7.	Ballynahinch (Down)	1790
8.	Banbridge (Down)	1795
9.	Roughfort (Antrim)	1796
10.	Newry (Down)	1797
11.	Dromore (Down)	—
12.	Downpatrick (Down)	—
13.	Purdysburn (Down)	—
14.	Hillsborough (Down)	—
15.	Ballygaskin (Down)	—

The Four Towns Book Club

The United Irishmen also had a strong populist element, intensifying the emerging polarisation which the Volunteer movement had begun to excite. Popular Book Clubs had been founded in East Ulster in the 1780s, and these became United Irish cells in the 1790s. At these clubs and elsewhere, radical and republican propaganda was distributed, inspired by the popular success of Thomas Paine's *Rights of Man*. The United Irishmen cultivated an easily accessible style, well suited to public reading. They were able to bridge the oral–literate divide.

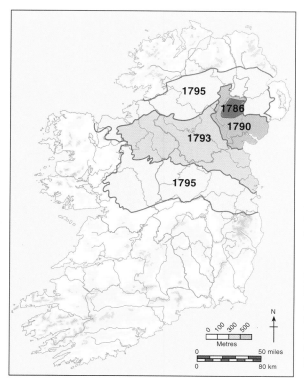

The Spread of Defenderism

The Defenders drew heavily on the Gaelic tradition of south Ulster, with its roots in both Jacobite rhetoric and a pervasive sense of the seventeenth-century shipwreck of the Catholics, felt most oppressively in an Ulster context. The French Revolution re-energised the latent millenarianism of a jaded Jacobitism, as vernacular republicanism fused in an unstable but energetic way with both Catholicism and a strongly developed sense of historically rooted social deprivation.

Aisling Ghéar

A county Cork manuscript of the 1790s is suffused with ideas of prophecy. The Aisling Ghéar (bitter allegory) draws equally on indigenous Gaelic tradition (traced back to Colmcille), on the Book of Revelations and on secular political predictions unleashed by the French Revolution.

Storming the Bastille

The fall of the Bastille generated considerable enthusiasm throughout Europe. It suggested that corrupt régimes everywhere might be in imminent danger of collapse. The French Revolution also energised the Catholics, prepared for the first time since the Boyne to stick their heads above the parapet of the Penal Laws. The early 1790s encouraged a more aggressive, abrasive stance: the old timid leadership of aristocrats and bishops was displaced in favour of a younger, more middle-class leadership. Stung by sneers about their self-assigned importance, the Catholic Committee organised the "Back Lane" Parliament of 1792, a nationally elected convention provocatively modelled on French precedent, and sitting at the Tailors' Hall in Back Lane, within a stone's throw of Dublin Castle and the Protestant parliament on College Green. The gauntlet was being thrown down. If the Catholic majority could not be accommodated within the existing narrow political structure, they would simply construct their own. The United Irishmen were also heavily – if discreetly – involved in the "Back Lane" Parliament and gained many recruits there.

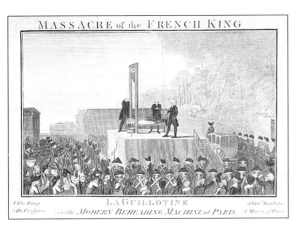

The Modern Beheading Machine at Paris

Inspired by Edmund Burke, conservatives tried to stem the tide of radical propaganda. They depicted the French as reverting to type – papist, despotic – with a violent new seam of insatiable barbarism, symbolised by the execution of their divinely-anointed king and the sadistic efficiency of the guillotine.

"Hitherto the Catholics of that country have proceeded with proper deference and submission to the laws, in their application for redress ... Sublimated, however, as men's minds are by the French disease, one cannot foresee what a continuation of oppressive laws may work upon the minds of the people and those of the Irish Catholics are much altered within my own memory and they will not in future bear the lash of tyranny and oppression which I have seen inflicted upon them, without their resisting or even complaining."

(Bishop Thomas Hussey)

"Political discussions have raised very much the expectations of the lower Catholics. They have been taught that the elective franchise will improve their conditions & they connect it with the non-payment of rents, tythes & taxes, the only objects of their consideration. They have in many parts assumed an insolence and shown a dislike to Protestants which occasions great alarm."

(Lord Lieutenant Westmoreland, 1792)

A War of Principle and Ideology

The Guillotine

By the early 1790s, it was becoming increasingly clear that the French Revolution would unleash a titanic European struggle between "democracy" and "aristocracy", between Republicanism and monarchy, between *liberté, egalité,* and *fraternité* and the *ancien régime.* Burke's emotional tirade, *Reflections on the Revolution in France* and Paine's caustic republican response, *The Rights of Man*, established the battlefield as one of ideas. As France and Great Britain moved inexorably towards conflict, it became apparent that this would be a new war, a war of principle and ideology rather than an old war of tactical and dynastic advantage. This new type of war would also place enormous demands on states and their citizens. The French mass mobilisation of highly motivated citizen-soldiers as opposed to reliance on a small standing army, redefined the very nature of warfare. The number of combatants and casualties escalated to unheard-of proportions, and the theatre of war aggressively expanded to embrace all of Europe. In these circumstances, once war formally broke out in 1793, the United Irishmen were immediately banned. Faced with state repression, the United Irishmen faced the options of shutting up or putting up.

Reflections on the Revolution in France

This satire on Edmund Burke suggests that his infatuation with Marie Antoinnette was not inspired by politics but inflamed by lust.

Prelude to Rebellion: United and Disunited Irishmen

"First up will carry the day"

"We will not buy nor borrow liberty from America, nor from France but we will manufacture it ourselves and work it up with those materials which the hearts of Irishmen furnish them with at home."

(United Irishmen, 1793)

Cave Hill

A momentous meeting took place on Cave Hill mountain overlooking Belfast in 1795. Here, the leading United Irishmen – Tone, Russell, Neilson, Hope, McCracken, Teeling – pledged never to desist from exertion until Ireland was free. Plans were laid for systematic revolutionary activity. Tone would enter France via America as United Irish ambassador, to seek a supportive French invasion. Neilson, Hope and Russell would continue reorganisation as a clandestine underground movement. McCracken and Teeling would oversee assimilation of the Defenders into the United Irishmen. This romantic Victorian version depicts Tone, Russell and Neilson agreeing this new departure.

War broke out between Great Britain and France in 1793. The United Irishmen, grudgingly tolerated in peacetime, were immediately banned as a potentially (if not actually) treasonable organisation. Concessions to Catholics, granted both to keep them from the clutches of the United Irishmen and to trade relief for recruits, stopped. An increasingly rigid conservative régime under William Pitt took over in Britain, which sided with the *ancien régime* in France, thereby exposing the shallowness of the democratic pretensions of the Glorious Revolution.

As the French Revolution degenerated into the Terror and as France itself showed signs of sweeping across Europe, not as a new army of liberation but as the old despotic conqueror, the radical enthusiasm of the 1790s sobered into a more pragmatic political assessment. The United Irishmen then faced the options of shutting up or putting up.

Faced with this stark question, United Irish opinion divided. The more conservative strand believed that the French were absolutely necessary to discipline the unreliable and potentially bloody Irish Catholics.

The more radical group argued for an indigenous insurrection, trusting to the good instincts of the Irish poor and their amenability to United Irish discipline. After the French had almost landed at Bantry Bay in 1796, United Irish radicals looked at the new troop configurations and saw how biased they were to the west and north, leaving Leinster virtually bereft of troops. A daring alternative was suggested: why not plan for a decisive strike in Dublin itself, independent of French help?

Bantry Bay punctured British complacency about French inability to breach her "wooden walls". After Bantry, a twin-track security policy had to be devised: one internal (to cope with the United Irish threat), one external (to deal with a possible French invasion). The internal strategy required troop dispersal. The external strategy demanded troop concentration, to cover the vulnerable "invasion" coastline from Waterford around to Derry. From 1797 onwards, under the shadow of the wider Franco-British conflict, Irish radicals and conservatives prepared themselves for the insurrection which all now saw as inevitable.

McArt's Fort

The United Irishmen consciously sought out resonant sites in Irish history. Andrew Nicholls (1804-1886), the most successful Belfast painter of the nineteenth century, painted the United Irishmen's meeting point at McArt's Fort, in its commanding location over Belfast Lough.

"I remember, particularly, two days that we passed on the Cave Hill. On the first, Russell, Neilson, Simms, McCracken, and one or two more of us, on the summit of McArt's fort, took a solemn obligation — which, I think I may say I have, on my part, endeavoured to fulfil — never to desist in our efforts until we had subverted the authority of England over our country, and asserted our independence."

(Theobald Wolfe Tone)

United Irish Seal

Henry Joy McCracken

McCracken, scion of two of Belfast's most respectable and respected Presbyterian merchant families, was a much loved figure in the United Irish movement. Tall, blonde haired, with an active social conscience, McCracken was an inspirational figure, who commanded great personal loyalty. In mid-1795 he travelled extensively in the Defender territory of south and mid-Ulster, laying the framework for the merger of the United Irish and Defender movements.

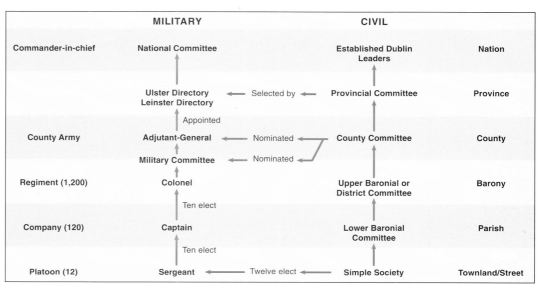

The United Irish Civil and Military Structure

The revamped United Irish organisation grafted a military structure onto the existing "civil" or political one. It cleverly balanced the need for a vertical command structure with horizontal popular mobilisation. It also took careful account of the intensely rooted territorial structures of Irish life, welding local loyalties to a wider national movement.

Theobald Wolfe Tone in French Uniform

Although he was an isolated newcomer, speaking broken French, Tone proved to be an extraordinarily effective ambassador in Paris. Urbane, sociable, quick on the uptake, Tone found himself at ease in cosmopolitan republican Paris. He was able to persuade an Anglophobic French Directory to undertake serious Irish invasion plans.

James Hope

Hope was a successful United Irish organiser, initially in Ulster and then in Leinster. After 1795, he was one of a number of key Ulster activists who were transferred to the Leinster theatre of operations. These included "The Emerald Pimpernel" William Putnam McCabe, John Metcalfe and eventually Samuel Neilson. Hope was especially influential among the working-class weavers, spinners, and artisans of the Liberties, the traditional industrial heart of Dublin. He was also resourceful, capable and utterly reliable, and had a contempt for half-heartedness or backsliding. He worked closely with his former employer and close friend Henry Joy McCracken.

National Archives

THE CRY OF THE POOR FOR BREAD, TO LORDS OF MANORS, AND OTHER MEN OF LANDED PROPERTY!!!

OH! Lords of Manors, and other men of Landed property, as you have monopolized to yourselves the land, its vegetations, and its game, the fish of rivers, and the fowls of Heaven,* can you afford no more than 1lb. 12oz. of very bad, wet, musty, and adulterated bread for 4d? and butter, cheese, and flesh, proportionably dear, by which, your worships not only diminish the value of labour, but make it scarcer, in proportion as you advance the value of provisions, rent, and taxes. In the present condition of things, can the labourer, who cultivates your land with the sweat of his brow, the working manufacturer or the mechanic, support himself, a wife, and 5 or 6 children? How much comfort do you extort from their misery, by places, offices, and pensions, and consume in idleness, dissipation, riot, and luxury?

AND will you do more, will you hunt, will you kill, and will you destroy with the sword, as well as with hunger, your thus degraded and miserable brothers, if they cry to you for bread? Or how can you, Parliament men, insult their feelings and affliction, by representing them in your speeches, as comfortable and happy, if thousands are literally in a state of starvation?

CITIZENS, Soldiers, Militia, Fencibles, Countrymen, and Kindred Blood, will you kill your brothers, from whose bowels, and rags, hitherto the principal part of your miserable pay has been extorted?

OH! Ireland, if thy rulers are deaf to thy cry for bread, despair not, neither destroy thyself by party or intestine divisions! Only make one united appeal to God, who cannot be an unconcerned spectator of the involuntary slavery of any of his offspring. Will thy freedom. And speak thy will with one voice, and his irresistible power to affect it, may be on the wings of the wind!

* The Game Laws.

The Republic

The Cry of the Poor for Bread

The need for mass mobilisation encouraged the United Irishmen to look more seriously at the politics of Irish poverty. The new departure in 1795 involved a much more self-conscious social radicalism (promoted by Russell, Neilson, McCracken, Hope and Tone), which explicitly addressed issues of living standards, taxes, tithes, rents and wages – the grievances of the rural poor and the agrarian secret societies. "The Cry of the Poor for Bread", written by John Citizen Burk, is a good example of this social radicalism. The Cork-born Burk had been expelled from Trinity College for atheism and was a well-known radical in the Liberties, the traditional working-class area of Dublin.

Cread

The United Irishmen were skilled satirists. This "Cread" lampoons John Beresford and John Fitzgibbon ("The Holy Earl of Clare") while parodying the Apostle's Creed. These clever squibs were influential in popularising the United Irishmen's cause, in effect bringing the republic to the village.

CREAD.

I believe in JOHN BERESFORD, the Father Almighty of the Revenue, Creator of the North Wall, the OTTIWELL JOBB and the Coal Tax, and in his true Son JOHN CLAUDIUS, who was conceived in the spirit of the Chancellor, born of the Virgin Custom-house, suffered under Earl FITZWILLIAM, was stigmatized, spurned at and dismissed.

The third week he arose again, ascendeth into the cabinet and sitteth on the right hand of his Father, from whence he shall come to Judge by Court Martial both the Quick and the Dead, those who are to be Hanged and those whose Fortunes are to be Confiscated, I believe in the Holy Earl of Clare, in the Holy Orange Lodges, in the Communion of Commissioners, in the forgiveness of Sins by acts of Indemnity, in the Resurrection of the Protestant Ascendancy and Jobbing everlasting. Amen.

National Archives

in the Village

"[Arthur] Guinness — a brewer at James's Gate, an active spy. UNITED IRISHMEN will be cautious of dealing with any publican who sells his drink."

(Watty Cox)

TEMPLE

OF

SUPERSTITION.

AN

EPIC POEM.

BY

JOHN BURK, CITIZEN.

DUBLIN:
PRINTED FOR THE AUTHOR.
1794.

Temple of Superstition

A United Irish publication which appealed to a wide audience.

UNION STAR.

AS the UNION STAR is an official Paper, the Managers promise the Public, that no character shall be hazarded thro' its medium, but such as are denounced by authority, as being the partners and creatures of PITT, and his sanguinary journeyman LUTTRELL.

The STAR will be published occasionally, as new and notorious characters appear, which the Committee think proper to guard the SOCIETY of UNITED IRISHMEN against.

The STAR offers to Public Justice, the following detestable TRAITORS, as SPIES and PERJURED INFORMERS.

Those marked thus [*] belonged to *Societies.*

——— HOULTON—a thin, very ordinary, yellow fellow, about 20 years of age, wears a Naval uniform, lives in Ship-street, is son to Doctor Houlton, some years since a writer in the Freeman's Journal.

THOMAS WELDON—a tall fellow with long whiskers, serjeant in the Stephen's-green division, by trade a Sadler, lives in Nassau-street.

——— HARPER—a tall fellow, aukwardly made, serjeant in the Barrack division, is a publican, lives in Barrack-street, opposite the Horse Barrack.

BELL MARTIN—a middle size woman, about 30 years of age, dresses in black, appears like a servant, speaks a northern dialect remarkably broad, she is very yellow, goes about at night as a woman of the town, in which character she has made several captures, by the assistance of two soldiers, who are always within reach of her signals; she was brought from Belfast by Government, lived some time in the Castle, at present lives in Pembroke-court, Castle-street.

* WILLIAM FULLARD—a thin, fair complexioned fellow, about 5 feet 7 inches high, 20 years of age, is an apprentice to one Glazier, a mathematical instrument maker, Lazer's-hill, he is a very idle fellow, and to avoid working, has put himself under the care of Alderman Fleming, by whom he is paid as a spy and informer.

——— BARTOLI—an Italian Musician, about 5 feet 9 inches high, black eyes, is a private in the Stephen's-green division, lives in Dame-lane.

——— GUINNESS—a brewer at James's-gate, an active spy. UNITED IRISHMEN will be cautious of dealing with any publican who sells his drink.

——— HARWOODS—under middle size, black complexion, iron-mongers, lives in Mary-street, corner of Denmark-street.

——— IRWIN—about 5 feet 7 inches high, 30 years of age, by trade a glazier, lives in Moor-street.

——— KENNAN—about 5 feet 8 inches high, 50 years of age, keeps an artists warehouse in Fishamble-street, is a private in the Dublin Horse (so called).

——— MARTINS—two brothers, dresses genteelly, under size, dealers in horses, lives on Usher's-quay.

* ——— LACY—an old man, kept an iron-foundery in Lincoln's-lane, Arran-quay.

* ——— FERIS—a strong made villain, about 40 years of age, was an attorney and stripped of his gown for Perjury, lived in Green-street, at present in the Castle.

* ——— NEWELL—a very short fellow, about 26 years of age, after being notorious for a life of infamy, as cheat, perjurer and swindler, has been a convert to support the constitution; has destroyed the peace and happiness of many respectable families, by immuring their fathers and brothers, in Kilmainham and other Goals in this kingdom, on charges of High Treason; he is now protected by government, and at present resides with his father the Ascendency man. The name of NEWELL is well known in the counties of Westmeath, Meath, and Dublin.

——— PILSWORTH—a woollen-draper in Dame-street, a notorious spy and informer.

——— QUESTIEN—a dancing-master in Stafford-street, about 30 years of age, 5 feet 7 inches high, is a private in the Rotunda division.

——— WETHERALD—about 5 feet 6 inches high, contracted countenance, a stay-maker in Capel-street, lately expelled the Rotunda division for infamous practices, killed a poor man in a frize coat, some time ago, and was humanely justified, as the murdered creature, by his dress, appeared to be a defender.

W. B. SWAN—about 5 feet 9 inches high, woman's face, in-knee'd, occasioned by carrying a drum in his infancy, to which business he was reared, lives in Gt. George's-street, North, is an Inspector of Licenses, and a Justice of the Peace, is notorious for boasting of killing several poor unarmed people, by shooting and stabbing them. Alas! poor Irishmen, this infamous wretch is taken from the dregs of society, and rewarded with his Majesty's commission, for inhumanity.

——— CHARLES—a little fellow, a swadling saint, is a small grocer in Golden-lane, and a notorious spy.

* ——— HARWOOD—about 5 feet 10 inches high, lives on the Black-Rock road, is a collector of hearth-money, was a menial servant of P. Latouche, to which dignity he was raised from being a shoe-boy in Oxford.

(To be continued.)

Union Star

By mid-1797, the United Irishmen also clandestinely promoted a bitter broadsheet called the *Union Star*, published by the fiery Watty Cox. The son of a Westmeath blacksmith and himself a gunsmith, Cox blended social radicalism, an interest in Gaelic culture, a well developed sense of Catholic grudge and grievance and a biting satirical style. The *Union Star* had the tabloid quality of compulsive readability. Despite establishment outrage at this "assassination sheet", Cox's information was remarkably accurate, and he consistently identified key Dublin Castle spies like the prostitute Bella Martin, Edward Newell and Francis Higgins. Cox's warning on Guinness fell on deaf ears – one of the great failures of Irish history.

Mary Anne McCracken

Mary Anne McCracken (1770-1886) was a committed Presbyterian, political radical, social reformer, abolitionist and proto-feminist. In 1797, writing to her brother Henry Joy, she produced an incisive analysis, linking slavery in America, political slavery in Ireland, and the slavery of women in general.

County Down United Irish Meeting 8 June 1797	
Membership figures by barony	
Lower Castlereagh	– 3,000
Females	– 46
Kinellarty	– 1,000
Females	– 50
Secret Committee Report, 1798	

"Teapot Societies"

Women began to take a more active role in the United Irish movement. In Ulster and Dublin, separate societies of United Irishwomen were sworn, which were derisively called "teapot societies" by loyalists.

"Is it not almost time for the clouds of error and prejudice to disperse and that the female part of the Creation as well as the male should throw off the fetters with which they have been so long mentally bound?... There can be no argument produced in favour of the slavery of women that has not been used in favour of general slavery ... I therefore hope that it is reserved for the Irish nation to strike out something new and to shew an example of candour, generosity, and justice superior to any that have gone before them."

Mary Anne McCracken, 1797

"We think we cannot better occupy a small portion of our paper, than by recommending to the perusal of every mother who can afford leisure, a justly celebrated book, lately published by Mrs Woolstonecraft entitled A Vindication of the Rights of Woman. *The work abounds with ingenious observations, which do equal honour to the head and heart of the writer; it affords variety of judicious instruction, for the early management of the female mind, and frequently and pertinently corrects the assumptions of the* Tyrant man, *with a boldness and justice which demand admiration and convey conviction."*

(*Northern Star*, 22 December 1792)

Martha McTier

Women like Martha McTier, Peggy Monroe, Rose Anne McCracken, Eleanor Bond, Henrietta Battier and Mary Anne McCracken were prominent in radical circles.

"The Harp Newstrung"

**Denis Hempson,
County Derry**

**An Irish Harper
by James Barry**

The Belfast Harp Festival

This celebration in 1792 was a public expression of the United Irishmen's determination to give equal weight to the Gaelic as well as the English component in Irish culture. The United Irishmen, notably Sampson, Russell and MacNeven, saw the need to balance the particularity of national culture alongside the universal and cosmopolitan political ideals of the Enlightenment. The Harp Festival was a public gesture in this direction. Just as in the religious sphere, the United Irishmen sought to move beyond the disabling binaries of "colonial" and "native" and to assert the shared ownership of a rich Irish past by all the traditions of Ireland. The United Irishmen's miscellany *Bolg an tSolair* (1795) was a similar assertion of cultural appropriation, as was their adoption of the slogan "Éireann go brách" (Ireland Forever), their use of popular Gaelic tunes for their political ballads and their encouragement of the cult of Carolan as the national bard.

The Politics of Culture

United Irish initiatives deepened the politics of culture which had emerged in the 1780s, most publicly in the innovative volumes of Charlotte Brooke and J. C. Walker. The United Irishmen's adoption of the harp as a symbol should also be seen within this cultural context, as well as within its more obvious separatist reference. Popular depictions of brehon lawyers (right) also focussed attention of a gaelic and independent past.

Paddy's Resource, 1795

This United Irish songbook was enormously popular. Its frontispiece cleverly blends references to the French Marianne with the Irish Caitlín Ní hUlacháin, while also containing references to the Tree of Liberty and the chains of slavery. The pre-eminent image is of the harp. The United Irishmen sought to bring the language of sensibility, hitherto exclusively associated with females, into the world of politics, hitherto exclusively associated with males.

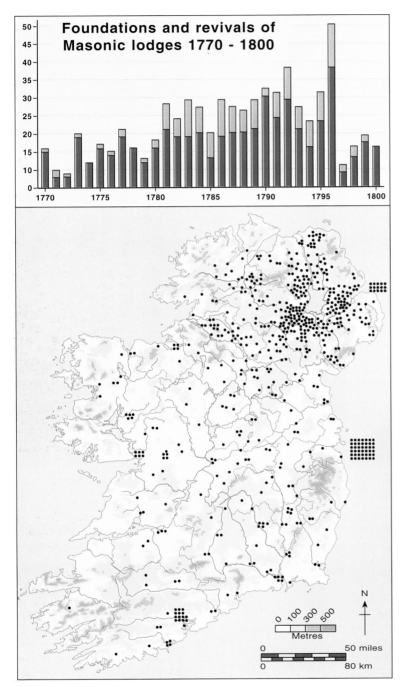

Foundations and revivals of Masonic lodges 1770 - 1800

Masonic Lodges, 1798

By 1798, masonic lodges were most intensely distributed in east Ulster, especially around the Lough Neagh basin. There was a close correlation between the distribution of Presbyterians, Freemasons and United Irishmen.

Freemasonry

The United Irishmen were originally conceived as a masonic secret society or "brotherhood of affection". Their oaths, tests and procedures were all grounded in masonic ritual. Because it was strictly non-denominational and because it endorsed speculative political theory relating to ideas of human perfectibility, masonry was amenable to political radicalism. In the 1790s, the United Irishmen used masonry as an organisational and recruiting mechanism. They were so successful that the government cracked down hard on it in 1797, forbidding the forming of new lodges.

"This society is the most perfect that ever existed: in it, there is no distinction of men by the language they speak, by the dress they wear, by the rank in which they are born, or the titles they possess: the whole world is considered but as one republic, of which each nation forms a family and each individual a member: under its banner, men of knowledge, virtue and urbanity unite, its members defend the whole by their authority and enlighten each other by their knowledge."

(Dublin book on Freemasonry, 1791)

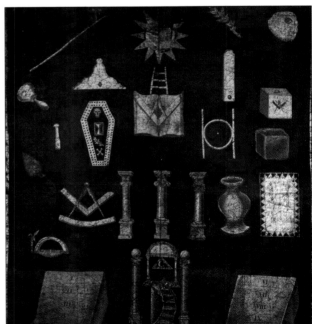

Freemason's Floor-cloth

"The French Disease"

"There is no longer a Catholic question: there is only the Irish question."

(John Keogh)

*"You natives of Ireland unto me now attend,
You have lost the worthy noble great would be a loyal Friend;
I planely say Fitzwilliam bold, who'd stand his Country's Friend,
Our Lord Lieutenant really thought the penal laws to mend."*

(A New Song Call'd The Lord Lieutenant's Farewell to the Kingdom of Ireland, 1795)

Fitzwilliam

The recall of Fitzwilliam as Lord Lieutenant in 1795 marked a turning point. A Burkean whig, Fitzwilliam had come to Ireland determined to grant Catholic Emancipation, to face down Beresford, Fitzgibbon and Foster, and to promote Irish whigs like Henry Grattan. When he began to implement this programme immediately, Prime Minister William Pitt sacked him, dashing Catholic hopes of full emancipation, and marking an end to legislative concessions to the radicals. After Fitzwilliam, Catholic activists showed a new willingness to join the United Irishmen. Bishop Thomas Hussey believed that the recall of Fitzwilliam left Ireland "on the brink of civil war".

EARL FITZWILLIAM.

John Thomas Troy, Archbishop of Dublin

The 1790s were a terrible decade for the Catholic Church. In Ireland, the situation was especially tense, as the Church was torn between the hardline sectarian stance of the state in support of "Protestant Ascendancy", the republican anti-clericalism of the United Irishmen, and the growing independence of their politicised congregations. Their public voice and acknowledged leader was John Thomas Troy (1739-1823), Archbishop of Dublin, who sought a cautious middle ground between a terrified Pope, a suspicious Dublin Castle, and a restless flock. Troy's political reticence and his efforts to establish a comfortable niche for the Catholic Church in a Protestant state enraged the radicals. Wolfe Tone called him "a great scoundrel", Watty Cox denounced his "pious alliance" with government, and Troy became for the United Irishmen the classic "Castle Catholic". Troy had the benefit of consistency; he excommunicated first the Whiteboys, then the Defenders and finally the United Irishmen. Troy's use of the arms of Dublin, and the motto "Archbishop of Dublin", was seen as a provocative gesture towards the Established Church, and indicative of Troy's hidden agenda of restoring the Catholic Church to its pre-Reformation position. Despite his impeccable political loyalism, Troy remained a figure of intense suspicion.

Maynooth College

Edmund Burke

Burke remained a staunch supporter of Catholic rights. He believed that the Penal Laws were an unnatural assault on Catholic rights: "One of the bodies was to possess all the franchises, all the property, all the education; the other was to be composed of drawers of water and cutters of turf for them." He lobbied extensively for the creation of Maynooth College.

Maynooth College

Backed by Edmund Burke, Hussey and Troy were able to persuade the state to fund a Catholic seminary at Maynooth. This was crucial to the Irish church because 90 per cent of their students had been educated in France prior to the Revolution. The project accelerated in the aftermath of the Fitzwilliam crisis and was denounced by the United Irishmen as a bribe to the bishops to keep silent. Henry Grattan claimed that the government was trying "to pervert religion into an instrument against liberty". After Maynooth, no bishop, with the exception of the maverick Thomas Hussey, publicly criticised government policy.

[We have chosen to communicate with Dublin Castle] not only in order to dispose government in our favour, but particularly in order to declare and clarify our true feelings at a time, unfortunately, when many of our people are acting foolishly and raving about a chimerical liberty and the false pretended rights of man. I have been pleased to find this government extremely satisfied with our conduct. Some democrats will raise a racket; but ... [we] are equally indifferent to their praise or censure. We are neither aristocrats nor democrats in the modern acceptance of party language. We have spoken as bishops, without taking notice of any party.

(Archbishop John Thomas Troy, 1793)

Bishop Thomas Hussey, President of Maynooth College

41

A L'ARMÉE FRANÇAISE,
DESTINÉE
A OPÉRER LA RÉVOLUTION D'IRLANDE.

RÉPUBLICAINS,

FIER de vous avoir fait vaincre en plusieurs occasions, j'ai obtenu du Gouvernement la permission de vous conduire à de nouveaux succès. Vous commander, c'est être assuré du triomphe.

Jaloux de rendre à la liberté un peuple digne d'elle, et mûr pour une révolution, le Directoire nous envoie en Irlande, à l'effet d'y faciliter la révolution que d'excellents Républicains viennent d'y entreprendre. Il sera beau pour nous, qui avons vaincu les satellites des Rois armés contre la République, de briser les fers d'une Nation amie, de lui aider à recouvrer ses droits usurpés par l'odieux gouvernement anglais.

Vous n'oublierez jamais, braves et fidèles Compagnons, que le Peuple, chez lequel nous allons, est l'ami de notre Patrie, que nous devons le traiter comme tel, et non comme un peuple conquis.

En arrivant en Irlande, vous trouverez l'hospitalité, la fraternité; bientôt des milliers de ses habitans viendront grossir nos phalanges. Gardons-nous donc bien de jamais traiter aucuns d'eux en ennemis. Ainsi que nous, ils ont à se venger des perfides Anglais; ces derniers sont les seuls dont nous ayons à tirer une vengeance éclatante. Croyez que les Irlandais ne soupirent pas moins que vous après le moment où, de concert, nous irons à Londres rappeler, à Pitt et à ses amis, ce qu'ils ont fait contre notre liberté.

Par amitié, par devoir, et pour l'honneur du nom français, vous respecterez les personnes et les propriétés du pays où nous allons. Si, par des efforts constans, je pourvois à vos besoins, croyez que, jaloux de conserver la réputation de l'Armée que j'ai l'honneur de commander, je punirai sévèrement quiconque s'écartera de ce qu'il doit à son pays. Les lauriers et la gloire seront le partage du soldat républicain; la mort sera le prix du viol et du pillage. Vous me connoissez assez pour croire que, pour la première fois, je ne manquerai pas à ma parole. J'ai dû vous prévenir, sachez vous en rappeller.

Le Général,

L. HOCHE.

Brest, le   année républicaine.

ÉTAT-MAJOR-GÉNÉRAL.

Au Quartier-Général de Brest, le 13 Nivôse, Ve. Année Républicaine.

ORDRE GENERAL,
Du 13 au 14 Nivôse, An V,
DE L'ARMÉE EXPÉDITIONNAIRE
D'IRLANDE.

BRAVES CAMARADES,

"A Protestant Wind"

"England has had the greatest escape since the Armada."

(Theobald Wolfe Tone)

General wonder in our land
    And general consternation;
General gale on Bantry Strand
    For general preservation.

General rich he shook with awe
    At general insurrection;
General poor his sword did draw,
    With general disaffection.

General blood was just at hand,
    As General Hoche appeared;
General woe fled through our land,
    As general want was feared.

General gale our fears dispersed,
    He conquered general dread;
General joy each heart has swelled,
    As General Hoche has fled.

General love no blood has shed,
    He left us general ease.
General horror he has fled,
    Let God get general praise.

To that great General of the skies,
    That sent us general gale,
With general love our voices rise
    In one great general peal.

"General Wonder in Our Land"

A contemporary poem cleverly caught the general mood of the loyalist population in Ireland.

Lazare Hoche

Lazare Hoche, the young but battle-hardened general, was the rising star (with Napoleon Bonaparte) of the French army. His allocation to the Irish invasion indicated how seriously it was viewed. If the French had landed, all were agreed that Cork city would have fallen, and no one could predict the subsequent fall-out. An exasperated Tone anxiously paced the storm strewn deck, within tantalising earshot of the Irish shore.

Bantry Bay

A formidable French fleet of 15,000 men reached Bantry Bay at Christmas 1796, the result of Tone's persuasive diplomacy. It was a stunning event. Although the fleet failed to land, due to atrocious Cork weather, its very arrival convinced even the most sceptical that the United Irishmen posed a real threat. The failure of their blockade to stop the French fleet leaving Brest was a huge disaster for the British navy. After Bantry Bay, no one could doubt either the inclination or the capacity of the French to reach Ireland in formidable numbers. It completely altered security assessments about the vulnerability of Ireland to invasion.

Bantry Bay

The loyalists of the "Bantry Garrison and Friendly Association" were quickly mobilised by the local landlord Richard White of Bantry House, to meet the French threat. The medal struck in their honour reads: "Deus afflavit et dissipantur" ("God blew and they were scattered"). Once again, a Protestant wind had saved England.

43

The Orange Response

The possible re-admission of Catholics into the political life of the state created considerable dismay among conservative Protestants. In Armagh which boasted itself as the most Anglican, Anglophile and "Independent" county in Ireland, the political divides over this issue also precipitated popular mobilisation. The Peep-O-Day Boys, forerunners of the Orange Order, emerged in the 1780s as a Protestant paramilitary force, engaging in early-morning punitive raids on Catholic houses suspected of possessing arms. Some liberal Armagh Volunteer corps had begun admitting Catholics as members and possession of firearms (more than the vote) was the badge of citizenship in the eighteenth-century world. In response, Ulster Catholics organised a similarly secretive protective force, called the Defenders. From the 1780s onwards, there was considerable rivalry, often degenerating into violence in mid-Ulster, which was the crucial transition belt between "Protestant" east Ulster and "Catholic" south Ulster. Tensions ran highest in Armagh, which had a clearly defined Anglican "north", Presbyterian "middle" and Catholic "south".

"As little could the Ethiopian be washed white as the Church of Rome be taught to endure an equal in power."

(Edward Newenham, 1795)

"We have thought much about our posterity, little about our ancestors. Are we forever to walk like beasts of prey over the fields which these ancestors stained with blood?"

(United Irishmen, 1791)

"[I hope] to increase the animosity between the Orangemen and the United Irishmen. Upon that animosity depends the safety of the centre counties of the North."

(General John Knox)

The Orange Wedge

After mid-1795, the United Irish merger with the Defenders proceeded apace. From the conservative perspective, this created the nightmare security scenario of the United Irishmen overrunning all of Ulster, and controlling the island north of a line from Dundalk to Sligo. In this context, the crucial buffer zone was in the Lough Neagh crescent, running from Dungannon to Lisburn, and centred in the cockpit county of Armagh. If the United Irishmen could spread unhindered down the Lagan valley, across north Armagh and into the Defender country of south Ulster, the north would effectively be lost. The founding of the Orange Order (the vulgar conservative equivalent of the Church and King mobs in England, with a vitriolic sectarian tinge) and the "Armagh expulsions" of late 1795 made sense in this context. The Orange Order was established in north Armagh, backed discreetly by local gentry and generals, to stiffen the loyalist backbone and to drive an Anglican wedge between Presbyterian/United Irish Antrim and Down, and Catholic/Defender south Ulster. The non-sectarian appeal of the United Irishmen was now met by a resoundingly sectarian Orange stance – with an emphasis on Englishness not Irishness, on the past not the future, and on disunited rather than united Irishmen.

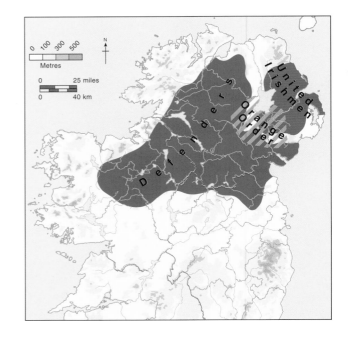

"To Hell or to Connaught"

"This is to let you know, Nancy McCanney, that your Brother, Hary McCanney was pleas'd to say that he had warrents and orders For Such & Such orange men in the Low Contry ... Be all the Secruts of hell your house Shall be Burned to the Ground. Both his Soul & your Shall Be Blwed To the Blue flames of hell. Now Teak this for Warning, For if you Bee in this Contry Wednesday Night I will Blow your Soul to the Low Hils of hell And Burn the House you are in."

(Orange threatening letter, Armagh, 1796)

"No news save that Great Britain is hanging the Irish, hunting the Maroons, feeding the Vendée, and establishing the human flesh trade."

(George Cumberland to William Blake, 1795)

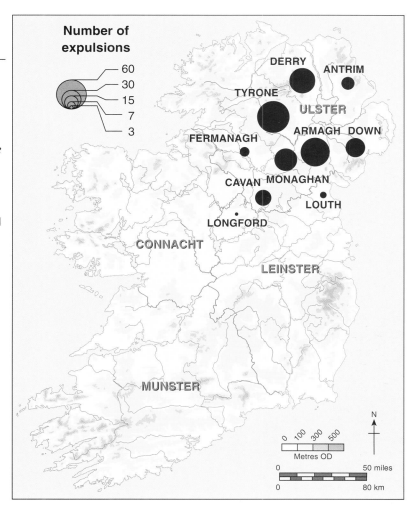

The "Armagh expulsions" of 1795-6

These involved sectarian assaults on Catholic homes in mid-Ulster, under the threat of being sent "To Hell or to Connaught". Five thousand Catholics were forced out, mostly moving to Mayo and Galway, but also scattering to Belfast (where they were sheltered by the United Irishmen), to Drogheda and Dublin, to Scotland and to America. There was a close correlation between the scene of the expulsions and the spread of the Orange Order. While publicly disapproving, Dublin Castle, briefed by local loyalists and generals, refused to intervene. This period marked the first deployment of raw sectarianism as a counter-revolutionary measure by the state.

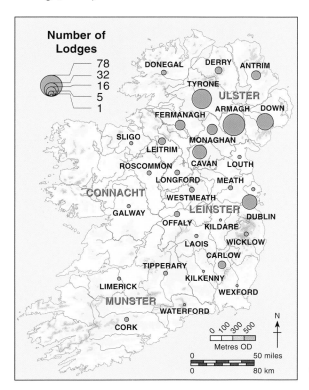

Orange Lodges, May 1798

Martial Law in '98

*"The country can never be
settled until it is disarmed
and that is only to be done
by Terror — by putting
certain districts under
martial law until all arms
and ammunition are
delivered up, and by
authorising the general
officers to declare war upon
property, until the
surrender is made. Arms
may be hid, ringleaders
may conceal themselves, but
houses and barns can
not be removed."*

(General Knox,
Dungannon, 1797)

General Lake

As well as covertly supporting sectarianism, the government also explicitly endorsed military over political responses to the security problem. The first systematic deviation from the rule of law came in the summer of 1795 when Carhampton personally headed a punitive campaign against the Defenders in the north midlands. He summarily dispatched 1,300 "suspects" to the fleets, using flogging and house burnings to extort information. The Carhampton campaign marked the supremacy of military over civil considerations in dealing with the mounting crisis. By mid-1797, with the Bantry Bay scare fresh in their minds, Dublin Castle launched a new hardline security offensive against the Ulster United Irishmen. Gerard Lake, a tough, hotheaded and politically naïve general, was dispatched north, with explicit instructions to use whatever military force was necessary to smash the Ulster movement. Lake's hamfisted "dragooning of Ulster" with house-burnings, arbitrary arrests and ill-disciplined troops, served only to alienate the province, and conveyed the impression of a rattled government who had increasingly lost control of the political and security situation.

Tap-room Politicians

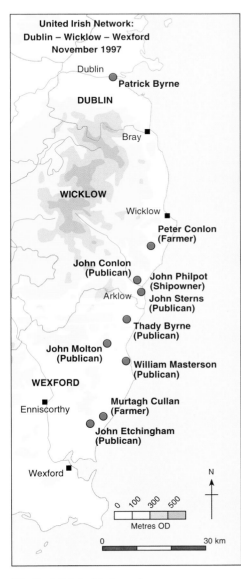

United Irish Network:
Dublin – Wicklow – Wexford
November 1997

Dublin

Patrick Byrne

DUBLIN

Bray

WICKLOW

Wicklow

**Peter Conlon
(Farmer)**

**John Conlon
(Publican)**

**John Philpot
(Shipowner)**

Arklow

**John Sterns
(Publican)**

**Thady Byrne
(Publican)**

**John Molton
(Publican)**

**William Masterson
(Publican)**

WEXFORD

Enniscorthy

**Murtagh Cullan
(Farmer)**

**John Etchingham
(Publican)**

Wexford

N

0 100 300 500
Metres OD

0   30 km

United Irish Network

From Dublin, the United Irishmen penetrated the surrounding counties. In November 1797, one such network stretched along the main Dublin–Wexford road, involving a series of public houses as nodes of United Irish cells.

Tap-Room Politicians (settling the affairs of the nation)

Paradoxically Bantry Bay strengthened the hand of those United Irish strategists calling for the indigenous revolutionary option. By mid-1797, the United Irishmen were heavily committed to building the organisation in Dublin and the surrounding crescent of Leinster counties, at the expense (if necessary) of the morale and momentum of their east Ulster core. Public houses like the Brazen Head in Bridge Street and the White Cross Inn in Pill Lane behind the Four Courts were important recruiting and organising centres for the emerging Dublin movement.

The Public House

In the public houses, the gregarious world of male bonding and convivial solidarity proved ideal recruiting grounds. In these settings, the United Irishmen used songs, toasts, jokes and public readings to spread the republican message.

Evoy's Forge

This photograph shows a famous '98 forge at Ballyshannon Lane in County Wexford. As the United Irishmen began to spread through rural Ireland, the blacksmiths were kept busy forging the simple but highly effective pikeheads.

Mounted and Dismounted Yeoman

The Yeomanry were established in 1796 as an auxiliary military force, recruited and officered at local level. Unlike the Volunteers, however, they were strictly controlled by Dublin Castle and initially they were deeply resented in Ulster as a merely mercenary force, or "an Ascendancy Army", as Henry Grattan called them.

Informers

Edward Cooke

The government developed an intelligence system, under the co-ordination of Edward Cooke, undersecretary of the Castle. As well as using the post-office, revenue and coastguard service, the Castle encouraged local loyalists to send information. Via threats or bribery, they also recruited a series of paid informers. Among the most successful were Leonard McNally, a trusted United Irish trial lawyer, Edward Newell, a Belfast-based miniature painter, and Francis Higgins, a Dublin newspaper proprietor.

What, have I not dared! and done! have I not Betray'd my COUNTRY.

Edward Newell

Newell turned informer in autumn 1796 and boasted of being responsible for the arrest of over 300 United Irishmen in the Belfast area. He was eventually "turned" again by the United Irishmen, and wrote a scathing exposé of Cooke's spy policy called *The Apostacy of Newell*, which was a propaganda triumph for the United Irishmen.

Town Major Charles Henry Sirr

The principal police officer in Dublin, he co-ordinated security policy against the United Irishmen and arrested many of them.

Francis Higgins

Stigmatised as the "sham squire" from a shady transaction, Higgins was able to use his work as a newspaper editor to recruit and run a team of informers in Dublin city. His most effective contribution led to the devastating arrest of Lord Edward Fitzgerald on the eve of the insurrection.

Leonard McNally

McNally turned informer to save himself from prosecution. As one of the United Irishmen's leading legal advocates, he had access to high grade intelligence. McNally remained undetected throughout a successful legal career – although in 1804, a banished United Irishman posted McNally a live snake from Botany Bay.

N.G.I.

Thomas Addis Emmet

"But if, which Heaven forbid! it hath still been unfortunately determined, that because he has not bent to power and authority, because he would not bow down before the golden calf, and worship it, he is to be bound and cast into the furnace; I do trust in God, that there is a redeeming spirit in the constitution, which will be seen to walk with the sufferer through the flames, and to preserve him unhurt from the conflagration."

(J. P. Curran on the trial of A. H. Rowan, 1794)

John Philpott Curran

William Sampson

United Irish Lawyers

As tension increased, the United Irishmen responded to the legal onslaught on them by politicising the issue of law and order. They used the increasingly coercive legislation of the late 1790s to put the law itself on trial, by extensively printing and circulating their trial speeches, and theatricalising the whole process. John Philpott Curran, William Sampson and Thomas Addis Emmet were competent lawyers and flamboyant orators. This strategy was highly successful in undermining the validity of coercive laws, in encouraging juries not to convict United Irishmen, and in deepening popular contempt for Dublin Castle and its legal policies.

50

Remember Orr

The most celebrated trial of the 1790s was that of William Orr in September 1797. An increasingly frustrated government stage-managed a theatre of terror in 1797, ranging from the dragooning of Ulster to the Blaris Moor executions of four Monaghan Militia men who had sworn the United Irish oath, to the execution of Orr. Briefed by Lord Castlereagh, the government had decided that an example be made of a leading Presbyterian United Irishman. The opportunity was provided by the trial of William Orr of Farranshane, a Presbyterian, Volunteer, freemason, *Northern Star* contributor and United Irishman. In a dramatic atmosphere, Orr was capitally convicted on disreputable evidence by a pressurised jury. Despite a massive campaign for clemency, Dublin Castle was flint-hearted. Orr's execution, and his exemplary conduct, galvanised Presbyterian east Ulster. He had a remarkable Republican and masonic funeral, and was quickly elevated into a Presbyterian martyr. William Drennan's angry poem "The Wake of William Orr" captured the mood of the moment and "Remember Orr" became the new slogan of the United Irishmen. Designed to cow Presbyterian east Ulster, Orr's execution succeeded only in further inflaming it.

William Orr in Carrickfergus Jail

Carrickfergus Jail

Orr's Execution at the "Three Sisters" on Carrickfergus Green

Barry Yelverton

"I hate those Yelvertonian tears."

(William Drennan on Orr's trial judge, who cried before passing sentence)

The Wake in Ballynure Meeting House

The Burial

The Grave

The Wake of William Orr
by William Drennan

Here our murdered brother lies —
Wake him not with women's cries;
Mourn the way that manhood ought;
Sit in silent trance of thought.

Write his merits on your mind —
Morals pure and manners kind;
In his head, as on a hill,
Virtue placed her citadel.

Why cut off in palmy youth?
Truth he spoke, and acted truth —
Countrymen, "Unite!" he cried,
And died — for what his Saviour died.

Hapless Nation — hapless Land,
Heap of uncementing sand!
Crumbled by a foreign weight,
And, by worse, domestic hate.

God of Mercy! God of Peace!
Make the mad confusion cease;
O'er the mental chaos move,
Through it speak the light of love.

Here we watch our brother's sleep;
Watch with us, but do not weep;
Watch with us thro' dead of night,
But expect the morning light.

Conquer fortune — persevere! —
Lo! it breaks, the morning clear!
The cheerful cock awakes the skies,
The day is come — arise! — arise!

52

Remember Orr

Orr Memorial Rings

Relics and mementoes of Orr circulated the length and breadth of Ireland. These bear the United Irish slogan "Éireann go Brách" (Ireland for Ever) and the mantra of the movement after his execution – "Remember Orr!"

Silk Rossettes

Irishmen! let us bear him in steadfast Memory:—Let ORR be the watch-word to LIBERTY! Let HIS fate nerve the martial arm to wreak the wrongs of ERIN.—and assert her undoubted claims:—

ORR.
and the
14th October.
1797.

The DYING DECLARATION
of
WILLIAM ORR, of Ferranshane

TO THE PUBLICK

My Friends and Countrymen,

In the Thirty-first Year of my Life, I have been sentenced to die upon the Gallows, and this Sentence has been in Pursuance of a Verdict of Twelve Men, who should have been indifferently and impartially chosen; how far they have been so, I leave to the County from which they have been chosen, to determine; and how far they have discharged their Duty. I leave to their God and to themselves ...

I am stamped a Felon, but my heart disdains the Imputation. My comfortable Lot and industrious Course of Life, best refute the Charge of being an Adventurer for Plunder: but if to have loved my Country, to have known its Wrongs, to have felt the Injuries of the Persecuted Catholic, and to have united with them and all other Religious Persuasions in the most orderly and least sanguinary Means of procuring Redress:— If those be Felonies, I am a Felon, but not otherwise.

To the generous Protection of my Country, I leave a beloved Wife, who has been constant and true to me, and whose Grief for my Fate has already nearly occasioned her Death. I leave five living Children, who have been my Delight — may they love their Country as I have done ...

I die in Peace and Charity with all Mankind.

WILLIAM ORR

Carrickfergus Gaol.
OCTOBER 5, 1797

SACRED
To the Memory of
WILLIAM ORR,
Who was offer'd up at Carrickfergus, on Saturday, the 14th of October, 1797:
an awful sacrifice to
IRISH FREEDOM,
on the *Altar* of *British Tyranny*,
by the hands of *Perjury*,
thro' the influence of *Corruption*
and the Connivance of
PARTIAL JUSTICE !!
O! Children of ERIN! when ye *forget* HIM,
his Wrongs, his death, his Cause,
the injur'd RIGHTS of MAN;
nor these revenge :—
May you be debar'd THAT LIBERTY he sought,
and *forgotten* in the Hist'ry of Nations;
or, if remember'd,
remember'd with disgust and execration,
or nam'd with scorn and horror!
No, Irishmen! let us bear him in steadfast Memory;
Let HIS fate nerve the martial arm
to wreak the Wrongs of
ERIN,
and assert her undoubted Claims :—
Let ORR be the watch-word to LIBERTY!

William Orr Memorial Card

The Rebellion in Leinster:
The Mighty Wave

"The heather blazing"

"Tis better to die like men in the fields than to be butchered like dogs in the ditches."

(Fr John Murphy)

"They who make half revolutions dig their own graves."

(St Just)

"A wet winter,
A dry spring,
A bloody summer,
And no King."

(Prophesy of 1798)

The French fleet concentrated the minds of United Irish strategists. Would a successful French invasion be necessarily a good thing? Given their recent ravages in the Netherlands, the Rhineland and Italy, would the French behave as liberators or conquerors? Eventually the radical alternative of an indigenous insurrection won out. On the evening of 23–24 May, the mail coaches leaving Dublin were seized as a signal to ignite the long-planned insurrection. The crescent of counties outside Dublin – Meath, Kildare, Wicklow, Carlow, Wexford – all rose as planned but the failure of Dublin to stage the necessary coup gave the Leinster theatre of war a haphazard, uncoordinated appearance.

Only in Wexford was the United Irishmen's first strike decisive and the stunning victory at Oulart Hill rose the county, as a mighty wave of insurgency swept across it. Hemmed in and under-resourced, the Wexford insurrection was finally crushed at Vinegar Hill.

The number of casualties was very high, the bulk of them civilians decimated by soldiers. Lake had issued a stern warning to his men on 25 May "to take no prisoners" and the mopping-up operation was brutal and unrestrained. As many as thirty thousand may have fallen in 1798, 28,000 on the popular side. The scale of the carnage was of European significance, indicating the extent to which the British state would go to crush internal dissent, within the wider context of the Franco-British war.

The United Irish Army fought bravely but ultimately lacked a commander-in-chief, a proper command structure, and munitions. The decision to fight pitched battles, as at Vinegar Hill, was misconceived. When they fought the "war of the flea", the United Irishmen were very successful. Their determination was always evident, nowhere more so than in the long march to Meath.

Dublin Castle breathed a sigh of relief when the rebellion was finally crushed. Castlereagh admonished an English friend: "I understand you are rather inclined to hold the insurrection cheap. Rely upon it, there never was in any country so formidable an effort on the part of the people."

1798 Battle Scene, Vinegar Hill

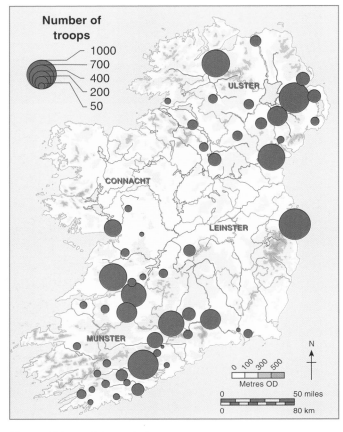

Number of troops

1000
700
400
200
50

ULSTER

CONNACHT

LEINSTER

MUNSTER

N

0   100   300   500
Metres OD

0   50 miles
0   80 km

Troop Dispositions 1797

After Bantry Bay, regular troops were concentrated in larger camps in preparation for the second coming of the French. Because a landing was expected somewhere between Lough Foyle and Waterford harbour, troops were deployed in a manner which would allow Munster, Ulster and Connaught to be quickly sealed off. With the exception of a large camp at Loughlinstown outside Bray, there were no major troop concentrations in Leinster.

The Strategic Plan

Responding to the new arrangements, United Irish strategists refined their indigenous plan. Instead of awaiting the French, the United Irishmen would develop their own insurrectionary capacity, based on Dublin city. A three-fold plan was developed. (A) Co-ordinated strikes to take over the capital. (B) An inner crescent of counties would support the Dublin rising. (C) An outer crescent would secure their own counties and prevent reinforcements arriving in Dublin from the big camps in the south, west and north.

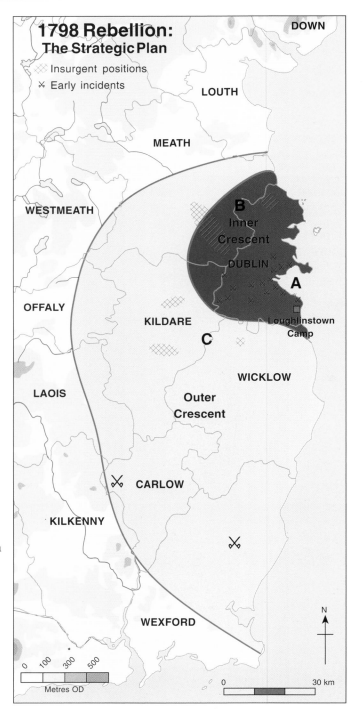

1798 Rebellion:
The Strategic Plan

⧄ Insurgent positions
✗ Early incidents

DOWN

LOUTH

MEATH

WESTMEATH

B
Inner
Crescent

DUBLIN

A

Loughlinstown
Camp

OFFALY

KILDARE

C

WICKLOW

LAOIS

Outer
Crescent

CARLOW

KILKENNY

WEXFORD

N

0   30 km

0   100   300   500
Metres OD

United Irish Numbers, 1795-1798

From mid-1797, the United Irishmen began to build their organisation in Leinster – especially in Dublin, Kildare, Wicklow, Meath and Carlow. The figures indicate a switch in emphasis from an Ulster-based to a Leinster-based organisation, with a focus on indigenous rather than imported insurrection. At the same time, United Irish numbers peaked in Ulster, with over 20,000 sworn in counties Down and Antrim. The earlier sharp increases in mid- and south Ulster indicate the successful merger with the Defenders.

County	July 1795	Sept. 1795	Oct. 1796	7 Dec. 1796	Early Feb. 1797	Late Feb. 1797	March 1797	14 Apr. 1797	May 1797	8 June 1797	11 Feb. 1798	19 Apr. 1798
Antrim	3,000	6,400	15,000	19,256	20,942	22,922	22,039	22,716	22,716	22,816		
Down	2,000	4,000	11,000	12,566	15,000	16,000	23,769	28,577	26,153	30,641		
Armagh			1,000	2,500	4,000	4,000	12,273	17,000	17,000	19,042		
Tyrone			4,355	6,500	6,600	6,860	12,169	14,000	14,000	12,594		
Monaghan			1,000	2,500	3,200	3,020	3,075	9,020	9,020	10,256		
Derry			3,696	8,000	10,000	10,000	10,000	10,500	10,500	10,500		
Donegal			2,000	3,000	5,088	5,000	9,648	9,648	9,648	3,264		
Cavan				800	1,000	1,000	1,000	688	688	3,807		
Fermanagh			1,500	2,000	2,000	2,000	2,000	2,000	2,000	3,000		
Louth			1,600	1,300	2,600	2,060	3,438	5,119	5,119	5,280		
Cork			1,600									
Meath				1,776	1,776	1,776		2,434	3,452	7,922	14,000	8,596
Dublin city								2,662	4,420	7,230	2,177	8,597
Dublin Co.								722	1,677	2,918	3,010	7,412
Kildare								850	1,530	12,703	10,863	11,910
Westmeath									2,000			5,250
Carlow											9,414	11,300
Kilkenny											624	6,700
Offaly											3,600	6,500
Wicklow											12,095	14,000
Laois											11,689	

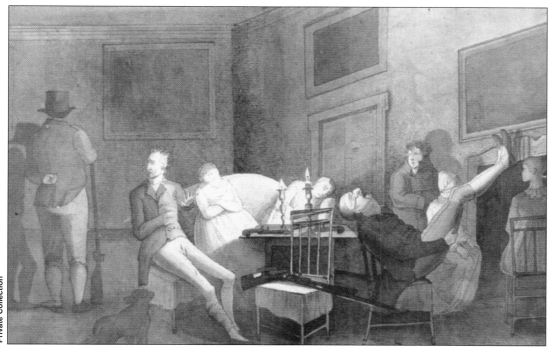

Private Collection

An Alarm by Caroline Hamilton

As the revolutionary threat visibly escalated, loyalists developed a siege mentality. Caroline Hamilton's drawing of the Tighe family of Rosanna in county Wicklow shows the whole family sitting up at night, behind heavily-shuttered windows and with armed yeomen in attendance. Compare the earlier painting by Maria Spilsbury Taylor (p. 23).

THE NEWRY GIRL

THE NEWRY GIRL

"The Newry Girl"

I met with Napper Tandy and I shook him by the hand.

And I asked him "how is old Ireland and how does she stand".

"'Tis the most distressful country that you have ever seen

For they're hanging men and women for the wearing of the green."

(The Wearing of the Green)

"A lady in Newry bragged about her green garters. The Ancient Britons tied her petticoats around her neck and sent her home showing her garters."

(Pelham to Pitt, 1 November 1797)

"Where is the man whose blood will not boil with revenge who sees the petticoat of his wife and sisters cut off her back by the sable of the dragoon, merely for the crime of being green?"

(John Edwards, Wicklow Magistrate)

"The Newry Girl"

At Newry, in an infamous incident, Scottish Fencibles slashed the green garters of a United Irish sympathiser and paraded her in an exposed situation through the town.

The Abercromby Crisis

"The army is in a state of licentiousness which must render it formidable to everyone but the enemy."

(General Abercromby)

An Irish Hug

This cartoon shows Fox and O'Connor embracing, prior to O'Connor's imagined transportation to Botany Bay as a convicted felon. In the event, only his companion, Rev. James Coigly, was convicted. He had been an influential organiser in mid-Ulster, and responsible for the Defender merger. Coigly was the last Catholic priest to be hanged by the British state on 7 June 1798.

General Ralph Abercromby

After a distinguished military career and at the height of his reputation, General Ralph Abercromby was appointed Commander-in-Chief of the Irish army in November 1797. He judged that Dublin Castle had exaggerated the security problem and made ruinous military decisions for reasons of political expediency. A tough disciplinarian, Abercromby was horrified at the disorder and confusion which he found in the army. By publicly seeming to back Grattan and the United Irishmen, Abercromby was viewed by Dublin Castle as a liability and they forced the resignation of what Fitzgibbon called this "Scotch beast". The sacking of this competent soldier-administrator once more placed security policy in the hands of Dublin Castle and the kitchen cabinet, who appointed the pliable Lake as the new Commander-in-Chief. Dublin Castle policy sought to force an early engagement with the United Irishmen before the French had once more landed. Lord Lieutenant Camden was an inefficient and dithering Viceroy, very much in the pocket of his kitchen cabinet – Cooke, Fitzgibbon, Foster, Beresford and Agar. The United Irishman Rev. James Coigly wittily called him "the degenerate Pratt", after his family name, John Jefferies Pratt. He sided with the kitchen cabinet against Abercromby, forcing his resignation and returning security policy into the control of Dublin Castle.

Lord Lieutenant Camden

London Corresponding Society, alarm'd, _Vide. Guilty Conscien

Pub.d April 20.t 1798. by H.Humphrey 29 S.t James's Street

"Here French faces, some with red caps and with crosses, and behind them an Hibernian variety of the Centaur genus, composed of a deranged man and a mad bull."

(Political nightmare of Samuel Taylor Coleridge)

The London Corresponding Society Surprised

With the Abercromby public relations disaster still fresh in mind, both Dublin and London were thrilled when the high-profile Arthur O'Connor was arrested in suspicious circumstances at Maidstone in April. After Lord Edward, O'Connor was the most high-profile United Irishman with very close connections to the English whigs Charles James Fox and Richard Brinsley Sheridan. Gillray's cartoon deals with fears of an Irish–French infection being transmitted into England by the Whigs. A meeting of the London Corresponding Society is being told of the Maidstone arrests. Clearly recognisable are Fox and Sheridan, both with strong Irish connections (Fox was a cousin of Lord Edward) and specific links to O'Connor.

"This land of tyranny"

It is the greatest happiness to you that you left this unfortunate country, now the prey of the Orange and Castle bloodhounds. Almost every county in poor old Ireland under martial law and the poor country peasants shot or hanged or basteeled without law or any form of trial; all our respectable and honest country men in the gaols of our kingdom, such as Arthur O'Connor, Oliver Bond, Edward Fitzgerald, Sweetman the brewer and several others, but thank God, that Irish men have resolution and can suffer more and will be free. I would send you a more full account only that I hope it will not be long until it will be known and praised throughout the whole world. Dear John, send no remittance to Ireland until you learn of her freedom, and then, when you do, your honest friends shall only receive the benefit. If the times are not settled before next August, I certainly will then leave this land of tyranny and seek a land of liberty. But for a man here to promise himself a single day to live would be presumption, for nothing but God can save us from what every Irishman must and will shortly endeavour to crush to the earth as they do us.

April 1798

The Devereux Letter

By the spring of 1798, the United Irishmen were still building their organisation to the requisite level in Dublin and Leinster while resisting intense government-inspired pressure. A Wexford farmer and United Irishman, Walter Devereux of Ballybrittas in Bree parish, wrote to his brother John in New York, indicating clear awareness at ground level in Wexford of the impending struggle.

John Devereux of Utica

After emigrating in the 1790s, he became a successful businessman at Utica in upstate New York.

The Arrests at Oliver Bond's House

Acting on his detailed information, Dublin Castle was able to arrest twelve leading United Irishmen at a provincial meeting at Oliver Bond's house in Bridge Street on 12 March. The Wexford delegate, Robert Graham of Corcannon, dallied with a barmaid at the Bleeding Horse in Camden Street, arrived late at the meeting and avoided arrest. As a result, no figure for United Irish recruitment in Wexford came into government hands, encouraging complacency about the county.

Thomas Reynolds as an Old Man

The government got a lucky break in March 1798 when they finally recruited a high-level informer in the hitherto unbreached Leinster organisation. Thomas Reynolds, the wealthy heir of a Dublin silk fortune, had set up in style as a country gentleman at Kilkea Castle near Athy. He was recruited by Lord Edward Fitzgerald as a suitably high-profile United Irishman but wavered in his allegiance and eventually agreed to become an informer.

N.M.I.

Lord Edward's Dagger

Lord Edward

N.G.I.

The Capture of Lord Edward Fitzgerald

A second hammer blow for the United Irishmen followed on 19 May 1798, with the arrest of Lord Edward Fitzgerald. He would have been the commander-in-chief of the United Irish army, whose very name would have galvanised popular support. His arrest, after a bloody struggle, led to him sustaining wounds which caused his agonising death a few days later on 4 June.

John

Henry

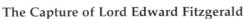

The Sheares Brothers

The death and imprisonment of key leaders caused frantic reorganisation in the Leinster Directory and also precipitated infighting. The impetuous Sheares brothers rose to prominence in the vacuum and decided on a fresh strategy of infiltrating the military. Their plans were betrayed by Captain John Armstrong of the Kings County militia, and the Sheares brothers were arrested and executed.

N.G.I.

"United Irishmen in Training" by Gillray

In England, there was incredulity that the United Irishmen could withstand professional troops in the field. Gillray mocked their military capabilities in this cartoon. Simian faced, bare-foot rebels attack a mock-up soldier, while a woman energetically grinds swords, under a pub sign "The Tree of Liberty", offering "true French spirit" to pike wielding, hard-drinking rebels. Gillray links bestiality, France and Ireland. These racial slurs intensified in the revolutionary period, when the comical, capering, politically-inept stage Irishman disappeared, to be replaced by these more menacing images.

Pike Drill

A traditional drill was used to train insurgents in 1798.

"Put the butt of the pike on the top of your brogue;
Measure it from there to the top of your waist;
Give your thrust forward, step back;
And be on guard again."

Cuir cos a' píce
le bárr do spáige;
Tomais as sin
go dtí do básta;
Tabair truslóg ar agaid
a's teana sátad;
léim ar gcúl
agus bí ar gárda.

Pikes

The favoured weapon of the insurgents was the pike, a weapon well-suited to mass insurrection. It was effective, cheap, easy to manufacture, simple to disguise by separating heads and shafts, and its use could be quickly learned. The pike was an excellent thrusting weapon, capable of breaking cavalry charges, with the pikemen formed firmly shoulder-to-shoulder in close set but deep files. The experienced French soldier, Miles Byrne, praised "the great power of the pike as a war weapon" especially at close quarters. Jonah Barrington declared it "irresistible in close combat", even against infantry. The '98 pike consisted of a plain head mounted on a shaft. Occasionally, a hooked projection was added at right angles below the base of the head, which allowed bridles to be slashed, and a backwards cut to be inflicted. The "halberd" style axe-blade was not used in 1798, but was widely available in 1848.

Seven Inches Deep

The effective use of the pike required courage, discipline, and skill in tight formations. Its use terrified opponents who had no experience of dealing with these "horrible weapons". The pike staff (8–12 feet) was grounded against the right foot, the point was inclined upwards, and the pikeman retained a double-handed grip on the shaft to face a cavalry charge. Joseph Holt, the capable Wicklow leader, taught his pikemen "to step in time, to face about, countermarch, wheel about, but particularly to disperse and form rapidly and to march in quick or double quick time".

> *"I know that they have me marked out. Look to the inhuman slaughter in Carnew, about nine miles from you and if the report of the butchery in Dunlavin be true, it is worse. Our jails are full of the best and the most beloved of our inhabitants and it may be our lot to be in company with them before tomorrow night."*

(Fr John Murphy to the men of Boolavogue)

Mobilisation in County Wexford

From 1797 onwards, the United Irish organisation had been unobtrusively spreading in north Wexford. When the signal came to rise in May 1798, they were able to mobilise quickly. After an early skirmish at the Harrow, they converged on the pre-arranged meeting point at Oulart Hill, on a low but commanding hill which dominated the area between the Slaney and the sea.

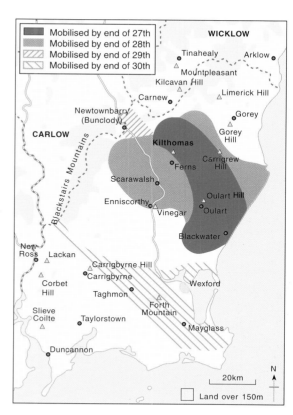

The Battle of Oulart Hill

Intelligently led by Morgan Byrne, Edward Roche, George Sparks and Fr John Murphy, the United Irish army achieved a shattering victory over the North Cork militia. Publicly Orange, and recruited from converts on the Mitchelstown estate, they were led by the arrogant sexual predator, Lord Kingsborough. The North Corks were much hated, especially after they introduced pitchcapping (an inflammable mixture of pitch and gunpowder was jammed on the victim's head and set alight). The victory was a stunning vindication of the pike's effectiveness against a cavalry charge on well-chosen ground. The enclosed Wexford countryside was dangerous for cavalry who could never get a clear sight of the enemy, and who were horribly vulnerable to well-executed ambushes by rebels familiar with the locality.

Supplement to the "Shamrock" of January 8th 1887

Oulart Hill

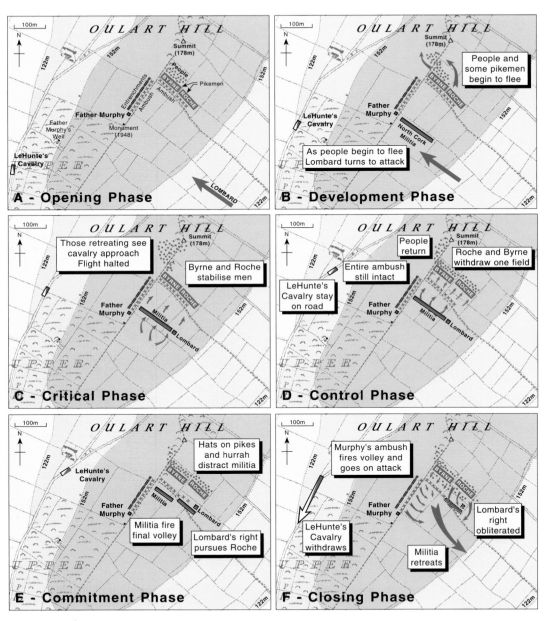

A - Opening Phase

B - Development Phase

People and some pikemen begin to flee

As people begin to flee Lombard turns to attack

C - Critical Phase

Those retreating see cavalry approach Flight halted

Byrne and Roche stabilise men

D - Control Phase

People return

Roche and Byrne withdraw one field

Entire ambush still intact

LeHunte's Cavalry stay on road

E - Commitment Phase

Hats on pikes and hurrah distract militia

Militia fire final volley

Lombard's right pursues Roche

F - Closing Phase

Murphy's ambush fires volley and goes on attack

LeHunte's Cavalry withdraws

Militia retreats

Lombard's right obliterated

The Battle of Oulart Hill

"Shame! Shame! Are you afraid of me because I wear [the red coat of a cavalryman]? No! You are not! It is not the man that you are afraid of. It is the red rag that frightens you. If you met them there below in a fair man for man, would their caps and red coats frighten you? Not at all. You would soon decide it with them."

(Morgan Byrne to the wavering insurgents on Oulart Hill)

70

Wexford United Irishmen

The Wexford United Irish organisation remained unscathed until the eve of the insurrection, with the arrest and torture of Anthony Perry, a leading Protestant United Irishman in the Gorey area. The pitchcapped Perry revealed the county command structure, leading to the arrest of Edward Fitzgerald, Bagenal Harvey and John Henry Colclough.

Private Collection

Beauchamp Bagenal Harvey

A leading liberal landlord and lawyer, he had been prominent in the Dublin United Irishmen until his return to Bargy Castle, his ancestral home in Wexford in 1797. County Wexford politics was riven between a conservative "Protestant Ascendancy" group, led by the Marquis of Ely and George Ogle, and a liberal, pro-Catholic whig group, centred on the Colclough, Harvey and Grogan families. Bagenal Harvey's interest lay in the civil rather than military side of the movement and he would have envisaged a legislative and administrative role after a successful revolution.

Edward Fitzgerald of Newpark

Adjutant-General for the county, with responsibility to lead the Wexford Army, Fitzgerald, from a wealthy farming and malting background, was typical of the rising generation of young, articulate Catholic activists who ran the United Irishmen in Wexford, in tandem with a liberal Protestant group.

John Henry Colclough

Esmond Kyan

From a Catholic gentry family at Mounthoward, Kyan was an experienced soldier and a very brave leader in the field.

Edward Roche

Edward Roche of Garrylough was an effective general in the Wexford army. Like many of the other leaders, Roche belonged to an old Norman landed family, and was a born leader of men.

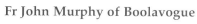

Fr John Murphy of Boolavogue

An obscure country curate when the rebellion broke out, he had wavered between loyalty to his church, and commitment to his increasingly United Irish congregation in the anxious spring of 1798. Faced with provocative and sectarian military tactics, Murphy eventually threw his lot in with his people rather than his bishop. He led the Boolavogue men in the initial skirmish at the Harrow and assumed a commanding position through his inspiring leadership at Oulart Hill and Enniscorthy. As a new recruit, Fr Murphy's success in the field undermined the existing command structure. Torn between Fitzgerald and Murphy, the Wexford leadership eventually pressured Bagenal Harvey into a military role as commander-in-chief, because he was an acceptable compromise candidate.

Private Collection

Private Collection

The Republic

The Battle of Enniscorthy

Fr Murphy's most daring victory was at Enniscorthy. Driven on by the momentum generated by Oulart, the United Irish army attacked the heavily fortified town on the Slaney, dominated by the massive castle. Murphy goaded a herd of cattle through the defences at the Duffry Gate, and poured pikemen through the breach. In tough hand-to-hand fighting, the insurgents gradually pushed the defenders of the town back towards the bridge. The decisive moment came when some of the attackers forded the Slaney above the bridge, creating the danger of encirclement for the garrison, who hurriedly abandoned the town and retreated to Wexford. This victory ensured the United Irish army would control practically the whole county and enabled the organisation of the Wexford Republic.

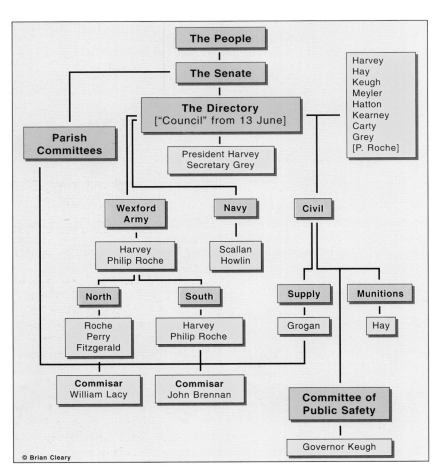

© Brian Cleary

The Republic of Wexford
31 May-21 June

The most remarkable achievement of the rebellion was the establishment of the Republic of Wexford – the revolutionary administration established by the United Irishmen based in Wexford town. A democratically elected "Council of 500" was created to run the county, with an eight-man Directory (four Protestant, four Catholic). It functioned remarkably smoothly, maintaining discipline and social order in the trying circumstances of attempted revolution. There was no damage to property and reprisals were remarkably restrained. The "Republic" ran the army, a fledgling navy, a food rationing and distribution service and a printing shop. Many of the town's Protestants cooperated with the Republic but this fact was quickly swept under a carpet of convenient amnesia after the Rebellion was terminated.

# of Wexford

COUNTRYMEN AND FELLOW SOLDIERS!

YOUR patriotic exertions in the cause of your country have hitherto exceeded your most sanguine expectations, and in a short time must ultimately be crowned with success — Liberty has raised her drooping head; thousands daily flock to her standard; the voice of her children every where prevails — let us then, in the moment of triumph, return thanks to the Almighty Ruler of the universe, that a total stop has been put to those sanguinary measures, which of late were but too often resorted to by the creatures of government to keep the people in slavery.

At this eventful period, all Europe must admire, and posterity will read with astonishment, the heroic acts achieved by people, strangers to military tactics, and having few professional commanders. But what power can resist men fighting for liberty!

In the moment of triumph, my countrymen, let not your victories be tarnished with any wanton act of cruelty; neither let a difference in religious sentiments cause a difference amongst the people.

To promote an union of brotherhood and affection amongst our countrymen of all religious persuasions, has been our principal object; we have sworn in the most solemn manner, have associated for this laudable purpose, and no power on earth shall shake our resolution.

To my protestant soldiers I feel much indebted, for their gallant behaviour in the field, where they exhibited signal proofs of bravery in the cause.

"To the People of Ireland", 7 June 1798

This proclamation issued over Edward Roche's name is a good example of the extent to which United Irish principles activated the rebel army. Throughout the rising, there were no attacks on women, children or political neutrals (like the Quakers).

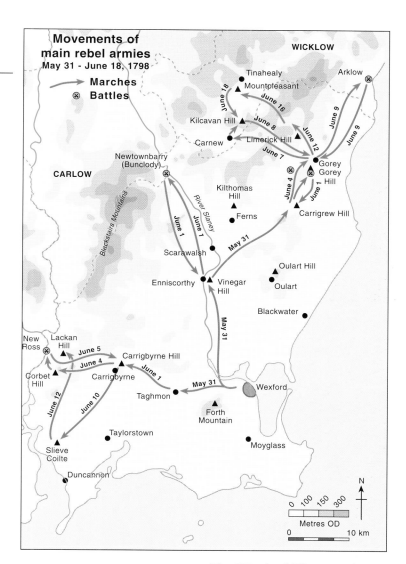

The Wexford Theatre of War

Once the Wexford army realised that the Dublin end of the plan had failed dismally, they were faced with setting new targets, beyond that of seizing their county and awaiting instructions. The topography of Wexford dictated that there were only three possible exit routes to spread the rebellion – at Arklow, Bunclody and New Ross. The Wexford men attempted to break out at each in turn.

73

The Battle of New Ross

Capably led by the young Bantry colonels, John Kelly of Killann and Thomas Cloney of Moneyhore, the Wexfordmen penetrated the town's defences and pushed back its garrison, only to lose the day, after hours of hard fighting. The clever counterattack backboned by reinforcements was led by the tactically astute General Henry Johnson. It was his finest hour and he later had himself painted with New Ross in the background.

Crawford Gallery, Cork

Bagenal Harvey at the Battle of New Ross

Massacre at Scullabogue

Retreating rebels from New Ross carried lurid stories of army reprisals as far as Scullabogue, a prison for loyalists (including Catholics) near the camp at Carrigbyrne. With the breakdown of control in the aftermath of the defeat, panicked and confused local units carried out a hasty reprisal against these prisoners, who were brutally burned in a barn. This sickening event occurred against the instructions of the United Irish leadership. Bagenal Harvey as commander-in-chief issued an angry proclamation next day, threatening immediate execution for all those who "killed, murdered, burned or plundered".

The Battle of Arklow

"I could not help admiring the clever military manner he kept his men manoeuvring, marching and counter-marching in the presence of the enemy. Doyle was stript, in his shirt, a red girdle or sash around his waist, an immense drawn sabre in his hand. He was at the head of about two hundred fine fellows, all keeping their ranks as if they had been trained soldiers and strictly executing his command."

(Miles Byrne on Matthew Doyle of Pollahoney at the Battle of Arklow)

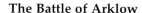

The Battle of Arklow

The most crucial battle of 1798 was at Arklow. If the United Irishmen had been able to break though here, the road to Dublin was open and the well-organised Wicklow and Dublin men, despite their earlier defeats, would have rallied to the cause. The Battle was long and arduous, and was only decisively tilted in the government's favour by the timely advent of reinforcements.

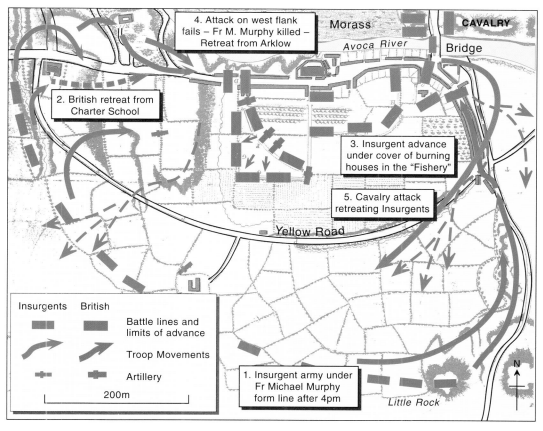

4. Attack on west flank fails – Fr M. Murphy killed – Retreat from Arklow

Morass

Avoca River

CAVALRY

Bridge

2. British retreat from Charter School

3. Insurgent advance under cover of burning houses in the "Fishery"

5. Cavalry attack retreating Insurgents

Yellow Road

Insurgents British

Battle lines and limits of advance

Troop Movements

Artillery

200m

1. Insurgent army under Fr Michael Murphy form line after 4pm

Little Rock

N

75

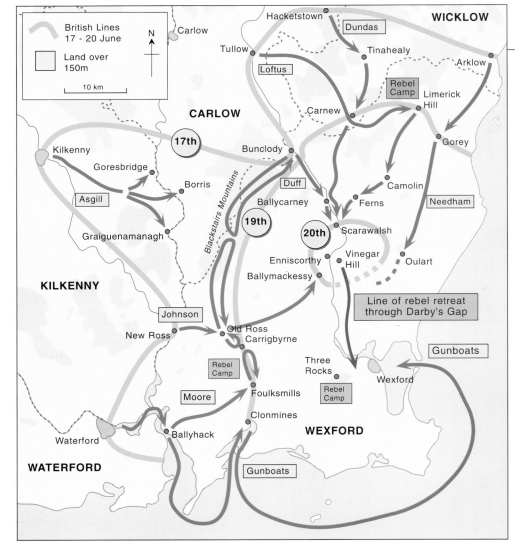

Private Collection

Defeated at New Ross, Bunclody and Arklow, their three natural exit points, the Wexford army was now hemmed in, on the defensive and increasingly aimless. The decision was made to fight one mighty pitched battle, from a base at Vinegar Hill,. in an effort to turn the tide. Others argued the case (but were outvoted) for a highly mobile, dispersed guerrilla campaign, a "war of the flea" in which local knowledge could be used to harrass, confuse and demoralise a static standing army sent into the field against them. As the United Irishmen fell back on the hill, a converging pincer movement was launched against them by General Lake, which created a slowly tightening noose around the Wexfordmen's necks. From the United Irish perspective, the Vinegar Hill decision was fatally flawed, because it conferred all the advantages on the side equipped with

artillery. At first light on the morning of 24 June, artillery fire rained cruelly down on the exposed hill. The frustrated pikemen were never able to close with their distant adversaries. For many hours, they withstood this murderous hail, but eventually began to break. One crucial factor now operated in their favour. General Needham (ever after ridiculed as the "late General Needham"), was expected to close the cordon around the hill on the south side at Darby's Gap, but was inexplicably slow in doing so. The pikemen, marshalled by Edward Roche, were able to retreat in good order through this gap and fall back on the Three Rock's camp above Wexford town. When Lake unleashed his cavalry on the hill, they mostly killed the camp followers who were slow to retreat – women, children, the wounded and the sick. The dead were cast into a pit at the base of the hill.

Hill

"The intention of the rebels in forming one great body was, that they might be able to cut off all the King's party and by that means clear the county of their enemies, for they were of opinion that so many of their friends were in arms in different counties that no more troops could be sent against them."

(United Irish Diary, Wexford 1798)

The Heroic Feats of Vinegar Hill,
a favourite new Song

Hibernia resolved upon Freedom and Fame,
Still laughs at those hacks that dishonour her name,
Her blood thro' her heroes she's ready to spill,
In valiant pike-fighting on Vinegar Hill,
Down, Down, Orange lie down.

The Orangemen boast in her blood they must wake,
In bulletten bombast and vaunting parade,
But Mountjoy their Champion fell there and lies still,
So long life and honour on Vinegar Hill,
Down, Down, Orange lie down.

The Welsh, Scotch and English, a fierce hireling crew,
Cajoled by their tyrants our sons to subdue,
But Scotch, Welsh and English have proved we can kill,
And cut them to pieces on Vinegar Hill,
Down, Down, Orange lie down.

With big proclamation our children they fright,
With curfews, alarm bells and pad-rolls at night,
We'd cure all such evils, with arcanum pill,
To scour them and bleed them on Vinegar Hill,
Down, Down, Orange lie down.

Their tall iron gates, palisades and walls,
Their loud roaring cannon, large bombshells and balls,
We're eager to meet them, from canon to quill,
At writing or fighting on Vinegar Hill,
Down, Down, Orange lie down.

Their despotic imposts and hard penal laws,
Their crowded Bastilles and curst Judicial flaws,
Be banished in time, or kept up if they will,
We'll make them repent them on Vinegar Hill,
Down, Down, Orange lie down.

Since then they're too restless and wayward to yield,
Our emigrant heros return to the field,
And, aided by Frenchmen, will crimson each rill,
With wardogs and blood hounds on Vinegar Hill,
Down, Down, Orange lie down.

"The Heroic Feats of Vinegar Hill"

Defiant but immobilised, the United Irishmen on the hill had virtually nowhere to go. They kept their spirits up by composing a new song which wickedly parodied the loyalist anthem "Croppies Lie Down".

These vivid scenes of Vinegar Hill and the Wexford campaign were sketched by William Sadlier, whose father had been in action there with the Royal Dublin Militia.

Private Collection

"The Long Barrelled Gun From the Sea"

The coastal Shelmalier men were practised gunmen from their wildfowling. They were among the most useful fighting men in the Wexford army. This later photograph shows one of the long barrelled punt guns in use on the Wexford slobs.

"Every bullet in that gun, General", he said, tapping the fowling piece, *"was worth three geese. I want to line them up."*

(Reply by a Shelmalier gunman to Thomas Cloney when asked why he was so slow in firing.)

The Capture of Colclough and Harvey

After the shattering defeat at Vinegar Hill, the United Irish leaders had to decide whether to continue the fight. Some fled. Bagenal Harvey and John Henry Colclough, with their wives, took refuge on the Saltee Islands off the coast of Wexford. They were betrayed and their hiding place discovered by the suds from their clothes washing. Both were brought to Wexford town, court-martialled, executed, decapitated, and their heads spiked over the courthouse.

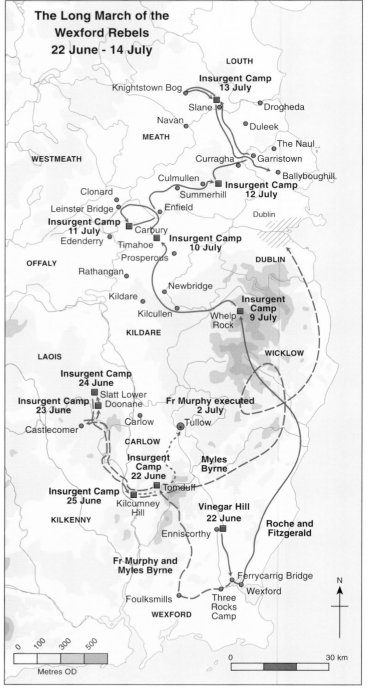

The Long March of the Wexford Rebels 22 June - 14 July

LOUTH

Insurgent Camp 13 July

Knightstown Bog
Slane
Drogheda
Navan
Duleek
MEATH
The Naul
WESTMEATH
Curragha
Garristown
Culmullen
Ballyboughill
Clonard
Summerhill
Insurgent Camp 12 July
Leinster Bridge
Enfield
Dublin
Insurgent Camp 11 July
Carbury
Edenderry
Timahoe
Insurgent Camp 10 July
OFFALY
Prosperous
DUBLIN
Rathangan
Newbridge
Kildare
Insurgent Camp 9 July
Kilcullen
Whelp Rock
KILDARE
WICKLOW
LAOIS
Insurgent Camp 24 June
Slatt Lower
Insurgent Camp 23 June
Doonane
Fr Murphy executed 2 July
Castlecomer
Carlow
Tullow
CARLOW
Myles Byrne
Insurgent Camp 22 June
Tomduff
Insurgent Camp 25 June
Kilcumney Hill
Vinegar Hill 22 June
KILKENNY
Enniscorthy
Roche and Fitzgerald
Fr Murphy and Myles Byrne
Ferrycarrig Bridge
Wexford
Foulksmills
Three Rocks Camp
WEXFORD

0 100 300 500
Metres OD

0   30 km

N

"Sure what good are they anyway? Didn't they piss on the powder in '98?"

(Wexford followers taunting Kilkenny during hurling matches)

The Long March (opposite)

The more realistic leaders believed (correctly) that surrender would bring instant death. From the Three Rocks, the United army split in two. One group, led by Fr John Murphy, made a long but fruitless march to Castlecomer, where they received little or no support. The miners were alleged to have urinated on their gunpowder. On their desolate return, the army melted away. Fr Murphy and his faithful bodyguard, James Gallagher, were arrested near Tullow by the local yeomen, and brutally executed in the square there. A second group, led by Roche and Perry, made an incredible long march via the Wicklow mountains to north Dublin and Meath. Failing miserably to garner local support their army also disintegrated, culminating in the execution of Fr Mogue Kearns and Anthony Perry at Edenderry in Offaly.

N.G.I.

Lady Pamela and her Daughter

After the death of Lord Edward Fitzgerald, the government extradited Lady Pamela to her native France, indicating their fear that a cult of martyrdom would build up around the widow.

81

The Rebellion in Ulster and Connaught: The Year of the French

"The Turn Out"

"Property must be altered in some measure: he who knew the recesses of the heart loved not the rich."

(Thomas Russell)

Belatedly, east Ulster, cradle of republicanism in the 1790s, rose in rebellion. However, the "Turn Out" as it was popularly called, proved to be a resounding failure. This was due to the failure of nerve on the part of its leaders and the unwillingness of the wealthier Presbyterians to support it in sufficient numbers. "The rich always betray the poor" was Henry Joy McCracken's caustic comment. Essentially, Ulster in '98 was a struggle between the Presbyterians (largely on the United Irish side) and the Anglicans (largely on the loyalist side). In the aftermath of the rebellion, the Presbyterians gradually turned away from their United Irish experiment and rejoined the Protestant consensus.

Just when it seemed that all was over, a French force of 1,100 men under General Humbert landed at Killala in the west. This small raiding party had been hastily cobbled together by the French Directory in response to news of the rising in Ireland. It landed on the west coast, rather than in the north or east, where the United Irish movement was not so strongly developed. The French were joined by a surprisingly large contingent of locals and achieved a stunning early victory over General Lake at Castlebar in county Mayo. Humbert then decided on a lightning march to Dublin but ran out of momentum at Ballinamuck. "Bliain na Francaigh" – The Year of the French – was at an end.

Henry Joy McCracken at the Battle of Antrim

83

Henry Joy McCracken

Henry Joy McCracken

While Leinster rose, Ulster remained quiet. The leadership there, devastated by a first wave of arrests in late 1796, followed by Lake's dragooning and a second wave of arrests in mid-1797, was untried, ill-prepared and unduly cautious (symbolised by the refusal to take the field of Robert Simms, the appointed leader in Antrim). The wealthier Presbyterians, especially in Belfast, now shied away from the rebellion they had for so long promoted. McCracken (for Antrim) and Henry Monro (for Down) had to step in as new leaders.

N.G.I.

84

"Pike Sunday"

Henry Monro

Monro, a lineal descendant of the Scottish general defeated at Benburb by Eoghan Rua (Owen Roe) O'Neill, was a Lisburn linen draper and committed republican. This entirely fanciful cartoon by Thomas Rowlandson was published in London on 1 July 1798.

"Pike Sunday"

Despite their hesitant start, the United Irishmen eventually took to the field in significant numbers, with at least half of their paper strength mobilising. On "Pike Sunday", 10 June, the Down men were mustered at the Creevy Rocks, where they heard an inspired sermon by Rev. Thomas Ledlie Birch, Presbyterian minister, Volunteer and veteran United Irishman, who preached on a text from Ezekiel 9:1: "Cause them that have charge over the city to draw near, even every man with his destroying weapon in his hand."

Men of Down are gathered here today, being the Sabbath of the Lord God, to pray and fight for the liberty of this kingdom of Ireland. We have grasped the pike and musket and fight for the right against might; to drive the bloodhounds of King George the German King beyond the seas. This is Ireland, we are Irish, and we shall be free.

Sermon by Rev. Thomas Ledlie Birch

The Taking of Ballymena Markethouse

The Down men were defeated at Ballynahinch. The Antrim men had a better run. They took Ballymena, where the decisive moment was the application of a burning tar-barrel to the market house where the loyalists had gathered.

"Like hens in byre-neuks"

"Then it was that a spectacle new and appaling for the first time presented itself: and presbyterian, churchman and catholic were seen to ascend the same scaffold and die in the cause of an indissoluble union."

(William Sampson)

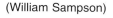

While close-leagu'd crappies rais'd the hoards
O' pikes, pike-shafts, forks, firelocks,
Some melted lead—some saw'd deal-boards—
Some hade, like hens in byre-neuks:
Wives baket bonnocks for their men,
Wi' tears instead o' water;
An' lasses made cockades o' green
For chaps wha us'd to flatter Their pride ilk day.

Donegore Hill by James Orr

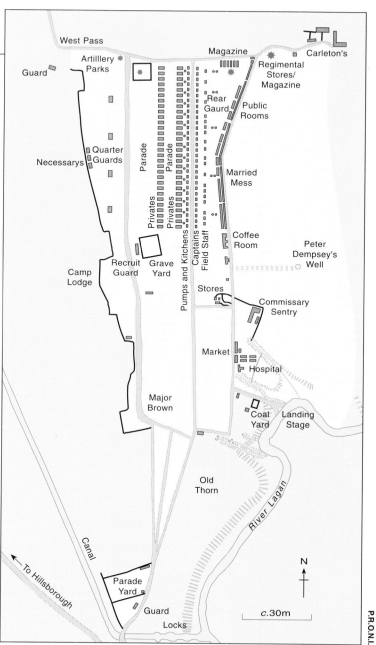

Camp at Blaris Moor

This was the major army camp near Belfast. It was deliberately located among the rabbit warrens near Lurgan to keep it isolated from United Irish infiltration.

87

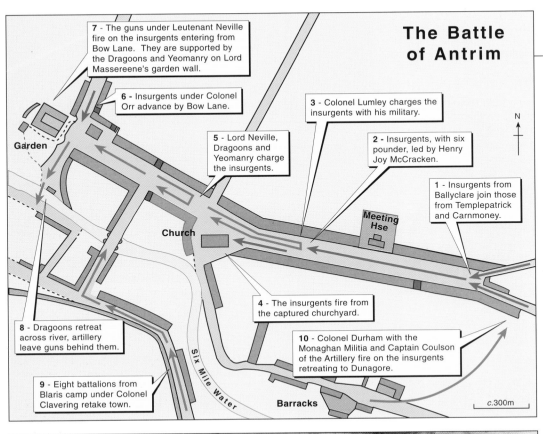

The Battle of Antrim

7 - The guns under Leutenant Neville fire on the insurgents entering from Bow Lane. They are supported by the Dragoons and Yeomanry on Lord Massereene's garden wall.

6 - Insurgents under Colonel Orr advance by Bow Lane.

3 - Colonel Lumley charges the insurgents with his military.

5 - Lord Neville, Dragoons and Yeomanry charge the insurgents.

2 - Insurgents, with six pounder, led by Henry Joy McCracken.

1 - Insurgents from Ballyclare join those from Templepatrick and Carnmoney.

Garden

Church

Meeting Hse

4 - The insurgents fire from the captured churchyard.

8 - Dragoons retreat across river, artillery leave guns behind them.

10 - Colonel Durham with the Monaghan Militia and Captain Coulson of the Artillery fire on the insurgents retreating to Dunagore.

9 - Eight battalions from Blaris camp under Colonel Clavering retake town.

Six Mile Water

Barracks

c.300m

The Battle of Antrim

The crucial battle in Ulster was at Antrim. Here, the United Irishmen, led by McCracken, launched a determined attack on a well-organised garrison. They swept down the main street, helped by their six-pounder cannon, but had to retreat to the shelter of the churchyard when met with withering fire from the Market House. James Hope with the Templepatrick men, was in the thick of the action at the churchyard, where their bravery and perseverance earned them the admiring nickname "The Spartan Band". General Nugent, alerted by the well-placed informer Nicholas Mageean of Downpatrick, had dispatched reinforcements. The arrival of the Monaghan Militia from Belfast, and eight batallions from Blaris Camp, turned the tide decisively against the United men, who retreated to their camp at Donegore Hill before dispersing.

Scene from the Battle of Antrim

"The abuse of power"

Viscount John O'Neill

Ironically, Lord O'Neill was among those who fell at the Battle of Antrim. O'Neill had been a leading liberal and a supporter of Catholic Emancipation. During the battle, some of the rebels had rushed O'Neill, dislodged him from his horse and piked him near the demesne wall. He was one of the best-known gentry figures to fall in 1798.

Francis Hutcheson

Many traced the Presbyterian involvement in 1798 to the effects of New Light philosophy, of which the founding father was Francis Hutcheson. Ulster born, he was a leading figure in training Presbyterian ministers at Glasgow University. He instilled Lockean ideas of the contract between rulers and ruled. "When the common rights of the community are trampled on, then as the governor is plainly perfidious to his trust, he has forfeited all the power committed. In every sort of government, the people have the right of defending themselves against the abuse of power."

NOTICE.

LIEUTENANT GENERAL LAKE having received Information that several Persons not belonging to the Navy, Army, Militia, or Yeomanry, appear dressed in Uniforms,—Notice is hereby given, that any Person so found will be considered as a Spy, and tried accordingly.

GEO. HEWETT,
Adjutant-General.

Adjutant General's Office,
Dublin, 30th May, 1798.

The Ghost of Henry Joy

'Twas night and the moon hid by clouds in the West
And the slave and the tyrant lay equal at rest;
Not a sound shook the earth but a noise from afar
And nothing remained but a quick shooting star.

Proscribed and proclaimed by the tyrants of power
I stole from my cot at the dead midnight hour
Where Henry's ghost met me, in green garments clad;
He smiled and addressed me while I shook with dread.

—Fear not, he says, tho' my features look wan,
It was I lately fell for the dear rights of man;
To give some insight I came from the skys:
Like the moon in full glory your cause shall arise.

The spirits (of those) who fell for the cause of reform
Shall lean from the clouds when the battle grows warm,
Strike terror and fright through the Orangeman's ranks,
Restore the green island, return the world thanks.

"It was then, indeed, the seat of Orange ascendancy and irresponsible power. To find a justice of the peace not an Orangeman would have been an impossibility. The grandjury room was little less than an Orange lodge ... I am now writing not only that which is well known to be historical truth, but that which I have witnessed with my own eyes."

(William Carleton on Ulster, c.1798)

"It is not in the poorest but in the richest parts of this kingdom that sedition and a revolutionary spirit prevail and first raised their heads. An extreme degree of poverty and distress will sink the mind of man, divest him of the courage even to complain and bury in silence himself and his sufferings."

(Rev. James Little)

Henry Joy McCracken

Attempting to escape to America, McCracken was recognised, court-martialled and executed in Belfast on 17 July. In a poignant last gesture, he gave a memorial ring inscribed "William Orr" to his mother, and died in a serene, composed manner. With him died the Ulster rebellion, but he bequeathed a legacy which survived in popular song. Henry Joy had taken to the desolate mountain moorlands behind Cave Hill, where he was tracked down by his devoted sister Mary Anne. McCracken consigned his four-year-old "natural" daughter Maria, to Mary Anne's care. Despite the frown of a moralistic and censorious Belfast, this respectable woman reared Maria as her own daughter in a loving family environment.

"Whole families sat up for nights in dread of being murdered by their Popish servants — it was confidently asserted in Faulkner's Journal *that an apothecary in Grafton Street had confessed to selling thousands of doses of arsenic to servants and cautioning heads of families to be on their guard — in the course of this unhappy contention, instances innumerable have been displayed how much baleful influence religious bigotry has had in cramping and contracting the intellectual faculties and blinding the understanding of men of the strongest natural powers of discrimination as well as poisoning the tender feelings and corrupting the hearts of the most naturally humane and honest men."*

(Diary of Richard Farrell, Dublin, June 1798)

Ulster
Museum

Mary Anne McCracken in Old Age

R. R. Madden, the great historian of the United Irishmen, was to praise "the fidelity of female friendship" as being his primary resource in tracking down the writings and the memory of the croppies. None was truer to the memory of the dead than Mary Anne McCracken. This valiant woman preserved the archive of both her brother Henry Joy and of her close friend Thomas Russell.

Pike Exercise by Brocas

This is a typical protestant image of 1798. A crucifix-wearing rebel wields a pike with rosary beads attached. He pikes an innocent child despite the entreaties of the mother.

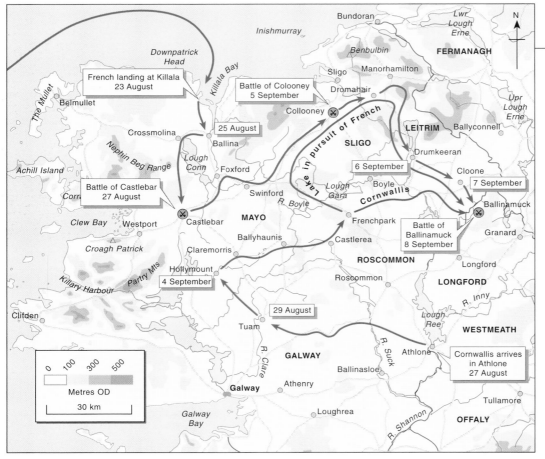

Map labels:
- Bundoran
- Lwr Lough Erne
- Inishmurray
- Benbulbin
- FERMANAGH
- N
- Downpatrick Head
- Killala Bay
- French landing at Killala 23 August
- Battle of Coolooney 5 September
- Sligo
- Manorhamilton
- Dromahair
- Collooney
- LEITRIM
- Ballyconnell
- Upr Lough Erne
- The Mullet
- Belmullet
- Crossmolina
- 25 August
- Ballina
- Lough Conn
- Foxford
- SLIGO
- Drumkeeran
- Cloone
- 6 September
- 7 September
- Achill Island
- Nephin Beg Range
- Lake in pursuit of French
- Lough Gara
- Boyle
- Cornwallis
- Ballinamuck
- Corr
- Battle of Castlebar 27 August
- R. Boyle
- Swinford
- Granard
- Clew Bay
- Westport
- Castlebar
- MAYO
- Ballyhaunis
- Frenchpark
- Castlerea
- Battle of Ballinamuck 8 September
- Croagh Patrick
- Claremorris
- ROSCOMMON
- Longford
- Killary Harbour
- Party Mts
- Hollymount
- 4 September
- Roscommon
- LONGFORD
- R. Inny
- Clifden
- Tuam
- 29 August
- R. Clare
- GALWAY
- R. Suck
- Lough Ree
- Athlone
- WESTMEATH
- Cornwallis arrives in Athlone 27 August
- 0 100 300 500
- Metres OD
- 30 km
- Galway
- Athenry
- Ballinasloe
- R. Shannon
- Tullamore
- Galway Bay
- Loughrea
- OFFALY

Map of Humbert's Campaign

Just when it seemed that all was over, a small French force landed at Killala Bay in the west, which had remained quiet during the long hot summer of 1798. The United Irish strength was in the English-speaking east coast, stretching from Antrim to Wexford, so the choice of landing place was not an inspired one. Humbert's expedition was a classic case of "too little, too late". Hobbled together at break-neck speed to support the Irish rising, it was essentially a raiding party with just over 1,000 men. By contrast, Hoche's Bantry Bay expedition had mustered almost 15,000 men.

Scene from the Battle of Castlebar

Barnageehy

Thousands did join and aided by expert local knowledge, Humbert executed a daring march high over the mountains through the gap of Barnageehy, and terrified the garrison at Castlebar.

Battle of Killala

Scene from the Battle of Castlebar

"The Races of Castlebar"

The sight of French troops so demoralised the loyalist troops that they fled precipitously – giving rise to the mocking tag "The Races of Castlebar".

Franco-Irish Fraternity

The French General Sarrazin embracing the corpse of a dead rebel.

Dublin Castle, 29th August, 1798.

ADVICES were received last Night from Lieutenant General *Lake*, by which it appears, that early on the Morning of the 27th the *French* attacked him in his Position near *Castlebar*, before his Force was assembled, and compelled him, after a short Action, to retire to *Holymount*. The Lieutenant General regrets that six Field Pieces fell into the Enemy's Hands; but states that the Loss of the King's Troops, in Men, has not been considerable.

General Lake's Despatch from Castlebar

His report concerning this ignominious defeat was economical with the truth.

"Bliain na Francaigh"

Cornwallis

Cornwallis, an experienced general, cautiously assembled a large force to meet Humbert. A Dublin observer was highly critical. "Ballinamuck, where the French surrendered, was not more, I believe, than fourteen miles from Mullingar – 800 men were taken without cannon nearly three weeks from the day of the descent and after penetrating almost to the centre of the Kingdom – notwithstanding they were pursued by our chief Governor at the head of 22,000 men – if they had taken a few hours less sleep they might have broken down the bridge over the Shannon and beyond the possibility of a doubt ... the capital of the Kingdom must have fallen into their hands."

Humbert Surrenders

Humbert surrendered personally to Lake, and the French troops were treated quite well. As they were dispatched to Dublin by canal, they astonished the locals by their rousing versions of *"La Marseillaise"*. Their Irish recruits did not fare so well. One in twelve was chosen by lottery and executed.

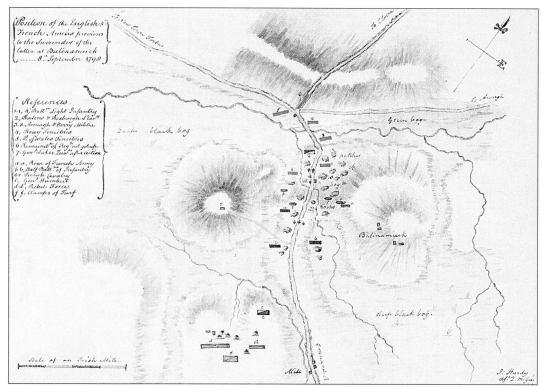

A Longford Rebel Surrenders

The Battle of Ballinamuck

Humbert realised that his only chance was a sudden, panic-inducing advance on the capital. He got as far as Ballinamuck in Longford, where his force was surrounded and forced to surrender unconditionally.

French Troops being Marched to Dublin

French Fleet off Tory Island

This French squadron was defeated by Sir John Borlase Warren on 12 October 1798. It consisted of the *Hoche* (a 74 gun vessel), eight frigates and a schooner, containing 3,690 men. Wolfe Tone, after fighting bravely, was arrested on the *Hoche* after the sea fight. He was recognised on the Quay at Buncrana by his old Trinity friend Sir George Hill and sent a prisoner to Dublin.

The *Hoche* in Tow of the *Doris*, Lough Swilly

Tone's death bed

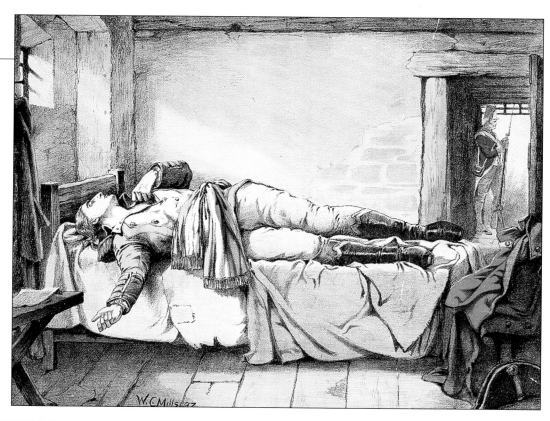

"What is there to live for?"
(Tone's last words)

Tone's Death Bed
by W. C. Mills

Theobald Wolfe Tone was captured off Donegal in yet another forlorn expedition. Court-martialled in Dublin, he died from self-inflicted wounds. Fitzgibbon sourly commented that he should have been hanged: "I would have sewn up his neck and finished the business." Tone had always shown unswerving commitment to the United Irish cause from his inception of it in 1791.

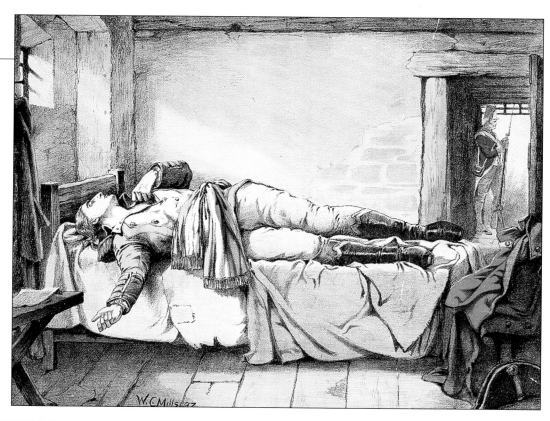

Princeton University

Passive Obedience
by James Barry

An anguished James Barry responded to the crushing of the 1798 rebellion in his drawing "Passive Obedience". The centre of the drawing is occupied by a convulsive void, with all the figures hurled to the edges. An angel comforts an innocent man, who recoils from the sickening violence before him – heads spiked on a castle wall, corpses being carried from a battle field, smoking ruins. The origins of the violence are depicted in the historical figures, including Edmund Spenser and King James I – judged by Barry to be historically complicit with the brutal and sectarian version of English colonialism in Ireland.

JOHN BULL ENJOYING GRAUNA.

"The Protestant Empire"

"Ireland is like a ship on fire: it must be either extinguished or set adrift."

(Lord Lieutenant Camden)

"I wish you would write a poem, in blank verse, addressed to those who, in consequence of the complete failure of the French Revolution, have thrown up all hopes of the amelioration of mankind and are sinking into an almost epicurean selfishness, disguising the same under the soft titles of domestic happiness and contempt for visionary philosophers."

(Samuel Taylor Coleridge to William Wordsworth)

"John Bull enjoying Grauna"

The Union was projected by the British as a solution to the divisions of Ireland. An impartial imperial parliament would rise above local sectarian factions, and Westminster alchemy would metamorphose the Irish (like the Scots after their union) into pliant British citizens.

The rebellion immediately became a political football, endlessly kicked about during the interminable Union debates. The propaganda war which followed 1798 ensured that the real principles of the 1790s were buried in a welter of recrimination and political point-scoring. Considerable energy was invested in portraying the 1798 rebellion as a mere sectarian and agrarian revolt of ignorant Catholic peasants, in an effort to detach Presbyterians from the emerging democratic movement.

It was distrust of Catholics which allowed the Act of Union to pass. Given the numerical dominance of Catholics in Ireland, conservative Protestants thought that it was wise to put them in a minority by joining the British state. Better to be among a confident majority of Protestants in the United Kingdom than to be an embattled minority in Ireland. However, acquiescing in the Act of Union was the end of Protestant Ireland's project of representing itself as "the Irish nation". In that sense, the Union was a humiliating defeat for them, as their vaunted Protestant parliament simply disappeared.

For Catholics, the Act of Union was initially welcomed. Their relief at being freed of their local taskmasters soon frosted over when, to placate Protestants, the Irish administration continued on strictly Protestant, and essentially Orange lines. In choosing this strategy, the British government ensured that Catholics would be turned from neutrality to hostility toward the Union, that local sectarian rancour would be institutionalised, and that the Catholic question would quickly become the Irish question.

Thus in the post-Union period, the enlightenment project of the United Irishmen simply stood no chance. Its secular and republican impulses were undermined and its universalist and international strains were domesticated.

The symbiosis of "nationalism" and "Catholicism" in Ireland hastened the withdrawal of Presbyterians from Repeal. The generous current of Irish nationhood, fed by many tributaries, as envisaged by the United Irishmen, was narrowed into a Catholic channel by the principal engineer of the new Irish politics – Daniel O'Connell.

N.M.I.

"The Babes in the Wood"

While the rebellion in its open phase had been crushed in 1798, pockets of resistance lingered on. The last group of Wexford United Irishmen called themselves the "Babes in the Wood". Led by James Corcoran, they were finally trapped and shot in Killoughrim wood near Enniscorthy, in 1804.

The Colclough–Alcock Duel 1807

Indicating the extent to which mainstream Protestant opinion in the county remained liberal, Wexford returned liberal candidates for much of the first half of the nineteenth century. This cartoon shows the duel between John Colclough of Tintern Abbey and William Alcock in 1807. The liberal Colclough, a United Irishman, was killed, and his funeral was the biggest ever seen in Wexford. It was the hardline conservative group, led by Ely and Ogle, that weakened appreciably in the aftermath of '98.

"The master of the mountains"

"The Wicklow Desperado"

Michael Dwyer at St Kevin's Cave

Michael Dwyer

The most celebrated survivor was Michael Dwyer from the Glen of Imaal in County Wicklow – the "master of the mountains". Dwyer knew the Wicklow mountains like the back of his hand, as well as being courageous, resourceful and ruthless. His highly publicised escapades were an acute propaganda embarrassment for Dublin Castle. In his most famous incident, Dwyer escaped from a house at Derrynamuck in the Glen of Imaal. His injured colleague, the Antrim man, Samuel MacAllister, sacrificed himself by brandishing his musket in the flaming door. Dwyer slipped out in the confusion, barefoot and almost naked, and escaped through the snow drifts.

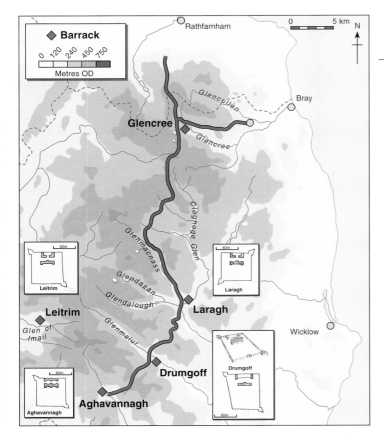

The Military Road

London and Dublin were so embarrassed by Dwyer's success that they decided to build a military road across the top of the Wicklow Mountains, from Rathfarnham to Aghavannagh, on the model of earlier efforts in the Scottish Highlands. It was built between 1800 and 1804, and was beaded by massive barracks which commanded the glens of Wicklow. In purely military terms, this road was a disaster. Had an invasion force approached from the Waterford Harbour area, the road would have provided a direct and easy route to the capital.

"The life of a Lord Lieutenant in Ireland comes up to my idea of perfect misery. I wish I were back in Bengal."

(Cornwallis)

"The violence of our friends, and their folly in endeavouring to make it a religious war, added to the ferocity of our troops, who delight in murder, most powerfully counteract all plans of conciliation."

(Cornwallis)

Cornwallis

When the Rebellion broke out, the fiction that Ireland presented only a security problem was abandoned. The Marquis Cornwallis, veteran of imperial wars in America and India, was dispatched to Ireland, both as Lord Lieutenant and Commander-in-Chief of the army – thus uniting the civil and military administrations. Cornwallis also had explicit instructions to carry an Act of Union and to prepare public opinion for it. Pitt had decided that the rebellion offered an unmissable opportunity to impose union on a terrified Ireland. Cornwallis immediately implemented confidence-building measures to woo Catholic opinion by distancing himself from the previous administration. He was hated by hard-line loyalists, who called him "Cropwallis".

"It is not an identification of people, as it excludes Catholics from the Parliament and the State: ... The union, then, is not an identification of the two nations ... it is merely a merger of the parliament of one nation in that of another; one nation namely England retains her full position: Ireland strikes off two-thirds. It follows, that the two nations are not identified, though the Irish legislature be absorbed, and, by that act of absorption, the feeling of one of the nations is not identified, but alienated."

(Henry Grattan)

Act of Union

"The Union. No Grumbling"

In this cartoon, Pitt is shown grinding down Orange and Green opposition to the Union, watched by the kilted Dundas.

"As we have seen smaller triangles erected in our public places, and stained with the blood of our countrymen, you are going to construct one great TRIANGLE from these three kingdoms, to which are to be tied the majesty and faith of the Irish monarch, and the inherent sovereignty of the Irish people."

(William Drennan to William Pitt, 1799)

"The Death of Erin"

Because they believed that the British Parliament would betray the staunchly Protestant principles on which Ireland had been run since the Boyne, the strongest opposition to the Union came from the Orange Order and hard-line Protestants. "The death of Erin" reflects the belief that the Union represented a murderous assault on the independence of the existing Protestant parliament, which alone guaranteed the security of its exclusively Protestant citizens.

The Act of Union by James Barry

Catholic opinion was led to believe that the Union would be accompanied by Catholic emancipation. James Barry's drawing reflects optimism in the new dispensation, in which an enlightened legislature, an impartial rather than sectarian-based administration and a cordial relationship between the islands would pave the way for peaceful settlement of the Irish problem. Irish Catholics would participate fully as citizens in the United Kingdom. The failure to grant Catholic emancipation until 1829 soured Catholics against the Union – which represented for them not a new beginning but a copper-fastening of "Protestant Ascendancy".

British Library

Private Collection

Union Street or Ease and Plenty

Anti-Union opinion was strongest in Dublin where the Union was perceived as a death-blow to the city's trade and self-importance, reducing it at a stroke from the second city of the empire to a petty provincial town. This 1799 cartoon depicts post-Union Dublin in rampant decay.

Society by Caroline Hamilton

This picture catches the utter boredom, the suffocating paralysis of post-Union Dublin. A comatose Dublin can scarcely keep itself awake in the yawning void created by the loss of its capital status.

*"I met murder on the way
He had a mask like Castlereagh"*

(P. B. Shelley)

*"So he has cut his throat at last! He!
        Who!
The man who cut his country's long ago.
So Castlereagh has cut his throat! The
        worst
Of this is — that his own was not the
        first.*

(Lord Byron)

Castlereagh

One of the principal architects of the Union.

The Foster Memorial

The great champion of the anti-Union cause was John Foster, hitherto a leading light in the kitchen cabinet which effectively ran Ireland, and a hard-line advocate of Protestant Ascendancy. Foster feared that a Westminster parliament would sell the pass on Catholic Emancipation. This monument to Foster's anti-Union stance was designed by a well-known architect, Richard Morrison. That it was never built reflected the fact that Foster's fears were groundless – the Union operated on staunchly Protestant principles.

109

"We are now in this country under a real republikan government and the best in the world ... Here I enjoy equal rights and privelidges as the Governor and I am an equal companion of our first rank whilst you must pour out your purse to landlords and whiper-ins and your hats in your hands at the same time."

(Letter of John Nevin, 1804)

Columbia and Hibernia 1796

This illustration shows Columbia welcoming Hibernia to the shores of America. The United Irishmen had a strong presence in America throughout the 1790s. The "Constitution of the American Society of the United Irishmen" was printed in Philadelphia in 1797. Branches existed all along the east coast – from Boston to New York to Washington and into Pennsylvania. The United Irish presence in the United States was swelled by thousands of refugees after the Rebellion, including many of their most talented members. They had their own newspaper – *The Shamrock or Hibernian Chronicle* – whose masthead depicted the American Eagle protecting the Irish Harp under the slogan "Fostered under thy wing, we die in thy defence."

Winterthur Museum

Private Collection

American 1798 Centenary Souvenir

This picture was produced in 1898 as a centenary tribute to the links between Ireland and America.

in America

Thomas Addis Emmet

William James McNevin

Edward Hudson

Robert Adrian

William Sampson

Thomas Jefferson

Skilled pamphleteers, newspapermen and spin-doctors, the United Irish *émigrés* were crucial to the emergence and consolidation of the Republican Party in America. They were credited with ensuring the election of Thomas Jefferson as US president in 1800. He was described by the United Irishman Watty Cox as "the first man for purity of character, talents and amiable manners in the republican world". By contrast, Cox described the Federalist George Washington as being "as cold as a dog's nose". He had refused to meet either the Irish republican Archibald Hamilton Rowan or the French

Leading United Irishmen in America

Among the leading United Irish figures were the lawyers Thomas Addis Emmet and William Sampson, the physician William James MacNevin, the dentist Edward Hudson, and the mathematician Robert Adrian. Denied a full role in political and intellectual life in the narrow sectarian ground of Ireland, these men flourished in the expansive republican milieu of America, where they quickly rose to the top of their professions. The United Irishmen were central to the American debate on national character, to the emergence of the party system and to the incorporation of ethnic minorities within a pluralist definition of American identity. As new citizens, they forged a new politics.

"General Devereux's Patriots of 1817"

The veteran United Irishmen constantly rallied to the cause of Liberty. In 1819, led by the Wexford '98 veteran John Devereux, and the Kildare United Irishman, William Aylmer, an Irish battalion sailed to Venezuela to assist Simón Bolívar in his efforts to free South America from Spanish dominion.

William Aylmer

Miles Byrne of Monaseed, County Wexford

Byrne joined the French Army, after fleeing to France in 1803, where he had a distinguished military career, rising to the level of colonel. Though he left Monaseed, Monaseed never left him, and he spoke with a broad Wexford accent until the end of his days.

Arthur O'Connor

The United Irishmen also remained active in France, where Napoleon had a special "Irish Legion" on constant standby for an invasion. Arthur O'Connor was made a general in the French Army in 1804 by Napoleon but he was never an active soldier. In 1807, he married Élise, only daughter of the French *philosophe* Condorcet, whose collected works he later edited. O'Connor purchased Mirabeau's old estate at Bignon and became a naturalised Frenchman in 1818.

112

Botany Bay

Joseph Holt

The Wicklow Protestant and United Irish General, Joseph Holt, was one of those transported to Botany Bay. His *Memoirs,* published in 1838, give a vivid account of life in the penal colony.

Mitchell Library, Sydney

Mitchell Library, Sydney

Vinegar Hill, Australia

Almost 500 United Irishmen were transported to Botany Bay. In 1804, they were accused of being instrumental in the Castle Hill uprising near Sydney, where 264 rebels tried to seize power, using the rallying slogan "Vinegar Hill". On the left of this engraving, the transported Catholic priest, Fr James Dixon of Wexford, is shown saying "Lay down your arms, my deluded countrymen". The rebel leader proclaims the old United Irish slogan "Death or Liberty" and is met by Major Johnson of the New South Wales Corps with the rejoinder "You Scoundrel, I'll liberate You". His quartermaster shoots a rebel at close quarters, while shouting "Croppy lay down".

The Remains of Mary Dwyer

She was the widow of Michael Dwyer. Having been buried since 1860 at Goulbourne, in New South Wales, she was exhumed in 1898. Remarkably, her body had not decomposed. She was reinterred with her husband under the massive monument erected at Waverley in 1898 – the largest '98 monument anywhere in the world.

Private Collection

Robert Emmet

Defeated as a mass movement in 1798, the United Irishmen reorganised as a much tighter and more centralised secret society, led by Robert Emmet. Emmet was born into a wealthy and well-connected medical family in Dublin. He entered Trinity College Dublin in 1793 but withdrew in protest at Fitzgibbon's purge of suspected United Irishmen in the college in February 1798. His elder brother, Thomas Addis Emmet, was already a leading United Irishman and Robert followed in his footsteps. By 1800, Emmet was already laying plans for a revived but more secretive and centralised United Irish organisation. He was studying military science, travelling extensively on the continent, and making overtures to France, including interviews with Talleyrand and Napoleon. By October 1802, Emmet was back in Dublin and began organising for a decisive coup in the city. He established depots in Irishtown, Patrick Street and Marshalsea Lane, and built a group of dedicated revolutionaries, mainly veterans from 1798. A complacent government was inactive in terms of preventing the conspiracy from reaching fruition. A premature explosion in one of his depots forced Emmet's hand and he took to the streets prematurely on 23 July 1803. The attempted coup was entirely abortive; the north, despite Thomas Russell's efforts, remained eerily quiet: the only serious incident was the killing of Arthur Wolfe (Lord Kilwarden) in Thomas Street. Emmet himself fled to Rathfarnham, then to the Wicklow Mountains and finally to Harold's Cross, where he was arrested by Major Sirr on 25 August 1803.

Viscount Kilwarden

"My lamp of life is nearly extinguished — my race is run — the grave opens to receive me and I sink into its bosom. I have but one request to ask at my departure from this world, it is the Charity of its silence — let no man write my epitaph ... when my Country takes her place among the nations of the earth, then, and not till then let my epitaph be written — I have done."

(Robert Emmet)

Emmet

Weapons of Robert Emmet's Uprising

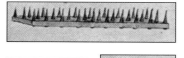

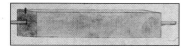

Speech from the Dock

His trial on 19 September elicited his famous speech from the dock, where the romantic Emmet made his impassioned defence which was to resonate down the echo-chamber of Irish history. This speech became one of the set-pieces of the Irish Republican tradition, notably its plea that Emmet's epitaph should not be written until Ireland was free. Ironically the first printed version of his speech was produced by the government, who emphasised instead his hostility to the French.

Green Street Courthouse

The Execution of Robert Emmet

This 1877 engraving shows the hangman holding Emmet's severed head, after his execution in Thomas Street, the initial site of his insurrection. He met his death with great dignity under St Catherine's Church. His body was buried in circumstances of such secrecy that his burial place has never been accurately ascertained. Underneath the romantic veneer, Robert Emmet was a determined revolutionary with a well-conceived insurrectionary plan.

Thomas Russell

"One of the most violent democrats on the face of the earth."

(Rowland O'Connor on Russell, Belfast 1795)

The Arrest and Execution of Thomas Russell

Thomas Russell was the other senior United Irishman involved in the 1803 Rebellion. Sent north to rouse the Presbyterians there, Russell met absolute apathy, was betrayed and executed outside Downpatrick Jail in October 1803. The failure of the north to support Russell was taken by Dublin Castle as reassurance that the Presbyterians had learned the lesson of '98, and had rejoined the Protestant consensus.

I was brave an' near to the edge of the throng,
Yet I know'd the face again,
An' I know'd the set, an' I know'd the walk
An' the sound of his strange upcountry talk,
For he spoke out right an' plain.
Then he bow'd his head to the swinging rope,
Whiles I said "Please God" to his dying hope
And "amen" to his dying prayer
That the wrong would cease and the right prevail,
For the man that they hanged at Downpatrick gaol
Was the man from God knows where.

(The man from God knows where by Florence Wilson 1918)

Napoleon

Louvre, Paris

The Coronation of Napoleon

Presbyterian distrust of France increased as Napoleon showed signs of reverting to despotic type – as in his assumption of the title of Emperor and his Concordat with the Papacy in 1801. From Armagh in 1799, it was reported that "The word 'Protestant' which was becoming obsolete in the north has regained its influence and all of that description seemed drawing close together ... the Orange system has principally contributed to this." Castlereagh reported with satisfaction: "The Protestant Dissenters in Ulster have in a great degree withdrawn from the Union [United Irishmen] and become Orangemen."

The KING of BROBDINGNAG and GULLIVER. (Plate 2.)__ Scene "Gulliver manœuvring with his little Boat in the Cistern." Vide Swift &c.

Napoleon and George III

A Swiftian slant on the French invasion threat, cutting Napoleonic pretensions down to size.

Female Politicians

This cartoon plays on British stereotypes of the French as sexually depraved.

Martello Towers

The threat of invasion led to the erection of Martello towers as an early warning system. These were strung along the vulnerable Irish coastline, including almost thirty in the immediate vicinity of Dublin harbour. Military white elephants, they added an exotic building type to Irish architecture. Thomas Davis described them as "a line of saucy absurdities drawn around our coast – a cordon of insulting folly encircling our native land".

Commemoration Dinner.

SUCH LOYALISTS as wish to commemorate the anniversary of the 21ft JUNE, 1798, (on which Day many good Subjects were fortunately rescued from the barbarous, tyrannical, and bloody Affaffins of the Town and County of WEXFORD), are requested to leave their Names at the Bar of the KING's ARMS, on or before the 19th Inftant, that Dinner may be provided accordingly.

IT is requefted, that no Perfon will prefume to dine there on faid Day, excepting thofe who have abfolutely diftinguifhed themfelves as loyal Subjects, in Order that no Controverfy fhould arife to injure the Happinefs which every well-difpofed Perfon fhould enjoy on that Day.

Wexford, June 11th, 1799.

CROPPY LYE DOWN!
Commemoration Dinner,
KING's ARMS, WEXFORD.
TICKETS, 5s. 5d. each.

"Croppy Lye Down"

Almost as it was taking place, the rebellion was being mythologised. This dinner took place in Wexford in 1799 on the anniversary of the battle of Vinegar Hill. Illustrating the tensions within the Wexford Protestant community, it warns that only those of the most approved loyalty should attend.

*In Wexford they made a most
   desperate stand,
And with fire and rapine disfigured
   the land,
Their massacred captives they cast to
   the flood,
The Slaney ran crimson with
   Protestant blood!
But vengeance pursued them with
   death and despair,
And the carcase of Harvey soon
   tainted the air.
Down, down, Croppies lie down.*

*Defeated by Lake, they rallied their force,
And into Kilkenny directed their
   course
By Murphy led on, o'er the Barrow
   they pour,
But hundreds were fated to pass it no
   more,*

*For Asgill attacked them again and
   again,
And three times five hundred lay
   dead on the plain.
Down, down, Croppies lie down.*

*Priest Murphy declared to the fanatic
   crew,
Who believed all his words as the
   Gospel were true,
No bullet could hurt a true son of the
   Church;
But the devil soon left the poor saint
   in the lurch;
For by some sad mistake, through a
   hole in his skin,
A heretic bullet just chanced to pop
   in.
Down, down, Croppies lie down.*

(Croppies Lie Down)

The Croppy Boy

Early, early last Thursday night,
The Myshall cavalry gave me a fright;
To my misfortune and sad downfall
I was a prisoner taken by Cornwall.
In his guard house then I was tied,
And in his parlour my sentence tried,
My sentence passed, and passed very low,
Unto Duncannon was obliged to go.

As I was going up the mountain high —
Who would blame me then for to cry —
I looked behind me, then before,
And my tender parents I ne'er saw more.

The captain told me he'd set me free
If I would bring them one, two, or three.
I'd rather die, or be nailed to a tree,
Than turn traitor to my country.

In Duncannon it was my lot to die,
And in Duncannon my body lies,
And every one that does pass by
Prays the Lord have mercy on the Croppy Boy.

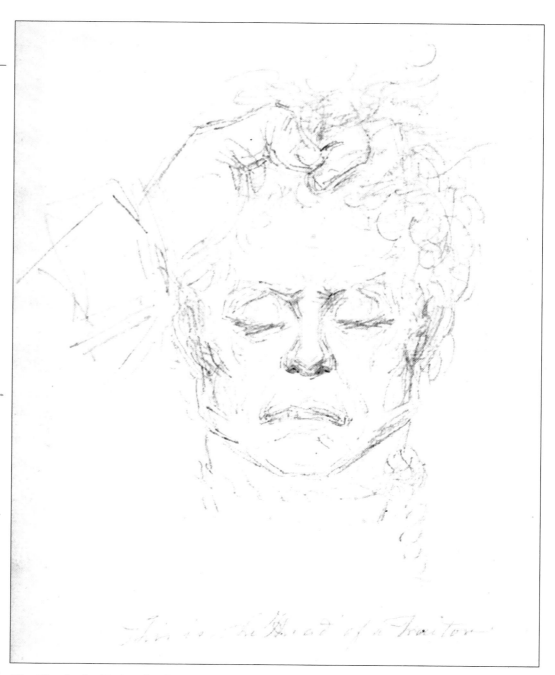

The Head of a Traitor by Brocas

Over 30,000 died in 1798, more than during the entire French Terror. These figures show the absolute significance of 1798 at the European level. Of the dead, over 90 per cent came from the United Irish side, illustrating the sheer scale of the suppression necessary to defeat their ideals. This drawing from the life by Brocas shows a hanged and decapitated rebel, bearing the caption "the head of a traitor".

O'Connell for ever and a day after
be der mighty powers but we'll be getting mancipation and whiskeypation
for nothing-blatherumskite blarney an botheration intirely
we'll all be Gintlemen this time every how at all

AN INDEPENDANT FREEHOLDER rejoicing at the TRIUMPH of the MAN
of the PAPAL

"The mere fact that it is not yet possible to speak or write of '98 without arousing a host of storms, passions, hopes and fears proves undoubtedly that the cause which introduced such a host of apostles and martyrs in that fateful year is not yet a lost cause, and is not regarded as such either by friends or enemies."

(James Connolly, 1898)

"When I was a boy, the Irish people meant the Protestants. Now it means the Roman Catholics."

(Lord John George Beresfsord, 1828)

An Independent Freeholder

O'Connell's mobilisation of the Catholic poor horrified British opinion who saw him as an irresponsible rabble-rouser. They portrayed the Irish poor as barbarians: squalid and savage, incapable of understanding political arguments.

The rebellion of 1798 occupied the place in the nineteenth-century imagination that 1641 had in the eighteenth century. There was a massive historiographical, political and literary response to the rebellion. The culmination of the literary tradition of 1798 was William Butler Yeats's play *Cathleen Ní Houlihan* (1902) which was to have a potent appeal to young nationalists.

Political interest peaked as the centenary loomed. Additional edge was imparted because it followed on the very zenith of imperialist bombast – the 1897 Jubilee Celebration of Victoria's accession to the throne. This had been enthusiastically marked in Belfast and Dublin. The nationalist response was to stage-manage the centenary as a riposte to those who believed that Ireland might comfortably settle into the Union niche. The Irish Republican Brotherhood was at the centre of the organisation of the centenary commemorations.

The centenary organisation brought together a coalition of nationalist politicians, helping to heal the Parnell split. It also acted as a platform from which was launched the independence movement of the early twentieth century. This nationalist takeover of the centenary generated a hostile unionist response and a repudiation of the Presbyterian contribution to 1798.

The Catholic nationalist version which dominated the centenary, 1938 and 1948 commemorations created the 1798 which people think they know. By getting behind these commemorations, 1798 can be re-opened as an event in the history of Presbyterians as much as in the history of Catholics.

The 1798 rebellion has remained a live issue in public debate in Ireland. From Eoghan Ó Tuairisc's novel *L'Attaque* (about the year of the French) to Stewart Parker's *Northern Star* (a play about Henry Joy McCracken) to Medbh McGuckian's *Shelmalier* (a collection of poetry exploring the parallels between the 1790s and the Northern Troubles), 1798 has continued to feed the literary imagination.

The ideals of 1798 need to be liberated from the straitjacket in which historians, politicians and propagandists have sought to confine them. The 1790s remain as a vision and an inspiration for the 1990s.

Repeal Meetings during 1843 attended by Daniel O'Connell

Monster Meetings

After 1798, Irish politics split into two fragments organised on sectarian lines – Unionist and Nationalist – which still dominate the political landscape today. In the first quarter of the nineteenth century, Daniel O'Connell rose to prominence as the charismatic leader of Catholic Ireland, driving the campaign for Catholic Emancipation. A former United Irishman, O'Connell repudiated their approach in pursuit of a majoritarian democracy, based on sectarian arithmetic. Catholic numbers would pave the road to power for the Catholic middle classes. His rise was facilitated by the destruction of an entire generation of political leadership in 1798 by execution, transportation or exile. O'Connell mobilised a monolith in which Catholic town and country, rich and poor, old and young were united. He was unwilling or unable to appeal to a broad Protestant base. His "Monster Meetings" of the 1840s were never held in Ulster and O'Connell presented himself as a leader, not of the Irish people, but of the Catholics. He was most successful in the heartland of Irish Catholicism, in big-farm Leinster and Munster.

The Temple of Liberty

This remarkable "Temple of Liberty, Learning and Select Amusement" was erected in county Antrim by John Carey as "a free gift to his country". It included statues of Grattan, Cobden, Kosciusko, Columbus, Washington and Wilberforce. The Presbyterians slowly retreated from the radicalism, espoused in this monument, in the first half of the nineteenth century. The fiery Henry Cooke emerged as a counterpart to O'Connell. The renewed emphasis on evangelicalism and personal salvation, anti-popery and political toryism helped to unite Protestant opinion and to return Presbyterian theology back into conservative channels. Yet, a strong liberal strand remained active within Presbyterianism, represented by Henry Montgomery, and drawn from the old United Irishmen. It only succumbed to the conservative embrace in the 1880s when Unionism presented a united front to the Home Rule movement.

"The unhappy men and women who fell victims at Scullabogue barn and Wexford Bridge have been the political saviours of their country. They live in our remembrance. Their deaths opened the eyes of many thousands in Ulster."

(Henry Cooke)

Cruelty of the Rebels at Wexford

Almost as they were happening, the events of 1798 were being recast in terms of memory. As with the politics, the memory also split into two fragments. In the Unionist one, 1798 was figured as a sectarian bloodbath, another chapter in the Protestant book of martyrs. 1798 was portrayed not as an attempt to overthrow reaction and replace it with enlightenment but as a rehearsal of the old sectarian animosities, cunningly disguised in the new French vocabulary. Sir Richard Musgrave was the principal Protestant historian of 1798. He presented it as the third element in a chain linking 1641, 1690 and 1798. He lavished particular attention on the alleged sectarian savagery of the Wexford rebels.

Massacre at Wexford Bridge

For Protestants, the iconic images of 1798 became those drawn by George Cruickshank (Dickens's illustrator) in the 1840s for Maxwell's *History of the Rebellion*. A gifted artist and technical innovator, Cruickshank's forceful but entirely fanciful drawings were enormously popular and touched a powerful Protestant psyche of persecution. They also mark the early Victorian emergence of racial stereotyping with the rebels portrayed as simian Celts.

CAPᵗⁿ SWAYNE
Pitch Capping the People of Prosperous

PLAN of a TRAVELLING GALLOWS used in the YEAR 1798.

Humbly dedicated to the Ancient & Modern Britons, by their dutiful Servᵗ W. Cox

Pitchcapping and Half-Hanging

In the Catholic/nationalist version, 1798 became a struggle for faith and fatherland in which the United Irishmen and the Presbyterians were air-brushed out of a picture increasingly dominated by the clerical collar of Father Murphy. In this approach, the rebellion erupted in Wexford as a wave of Catholic peasant rage and resentment against Orange and military oppression and was entirely devoid of political motivation. This tradition began with Watty Cox's *Irish Magazine* whose vivid cartoons by Brocas became an equally iconic (and misleading) visual memory of 1798 as Cruickshank's were on the Protestant side.

The Historians of '98

"It is hard for a man who did not live at the time, to believe or comprehend the extent to which mis-representations were carried at the close of our struggle; for, besides the paid agents, the men who flinched and fell away from our cause, grasped at any apology for their own delinquency."

(James Hope)

Historians

The historiography of the rising became equally partisan. In the immediate and bloody aftermath of 1798, the United Irishmen kept a low profile. In a damage limitation exercise, the less radical wing of the United Irishmen played down their role in organising the rebellion (as in the evasive accounts of Thomas Cloney, Edward Hay, Joseph Holt, William Farrell and Patrick Kelly). This initial series of misleading writings about 1798 lasted until after Catholic Emancipation had been safely secured.

Joseph Holt

R. R. Madden

By the 1840s, a second phase of interpretation began, which was much more explicit in acknowledging the revolutionary and republican principles of the United Irishmen and their pivotal role in organising the rebellion. This was explicit in the work of R. R. Madden, Thomas Davis (the crucial populariser of Tone) and the pioneer oral historian Luke Cullen. The indefatigable Madden was in essence a hagiographer of the United Irishmen. He always presented them in the best possible light.

Miles Byrne

His *Memoirs,* published in 1863, were the last by a direct '98 man. This 1859 photograph shows Byrne as an old man in his Parisian retirement. Published in 1863, Byrne's forceful account became a revered Fenian text and a problem for the institutional Catholic church. Given Byrne's highlighting of the leading role of the '98 priests in an oath-bound secret society, how did the church justify its strident anti-Fenian stance?

Áras an Uachtaráin

Father Patrick Kavanagh

This Wexford born friar provided an elegant escape route for the church from this Fenian hook. He developed a faith and fatherland model of the rebellion as a Catholic crusade devoid of United Irish influence. It was provoked not organised, its spread was spontaneous and the United Irishmen never organised in Wexford. This trumped the Miles Byrne/Fenian card; oath/secret societies were a liability, riddled by spies and informers. Appearing originally in 1870 but rapidly going through multiple editions, Kavanagh's *Popular History* salvaged the Rebellion for the Catholic church and dominated interpretation in the build-up to the centenary year of 1898. Kavanagh's text was written explicitly against the backdrop of the lurid church attack on the Fenians and obsessive clerical condemnation of secret societies. An important aspect of this was to focus on sensational stories of informers. W. J. Fitzpatrick, the eminent Victorian Catholic historian, stressed this aspect in his widely-read narratives of the spies and informers of 1798.

"Wexford rose not in obedience to any call from the United Irish organisation but purely and solely from the instinct of self-preservation ... the wild rush to arms of a tortured peasantry, unprepared, unorganised, unarmed."

(A. M. Sullivan)

Father Murphy at Vinegar Hill

In this Catholic nationalist version of 1798, the central feature was clerical leadership and the heroic role of Father Murphy. According to Kavanagh, the only genuine nationalist movement could be one led by Catholic priests. After Kavanagh, "the mighty wave" of Father Murphy swept all before it. This 1890s drawing shows the priest as the pivotal figure on Vinegar Hill.

The Memory of the Dead by Walter C. Mills

Father Murphy

In a remarkable incident in 1898, the painting of Father Murphy preserved at Boolavogue was sent to Dublin to be cleaned. The restorer added the Roman clerical collar over the priest's stock, to more fully identify him iconographically with the modern Catholic priesthood. The Catholic church had come full circle in a century. In 1798, Murphy's bishop had dismissed the rebel priests as "the very faeces of the church".

Private Collection

Private Collection

The Ancestral Home of John Kelly

This drawing is of the ancestral home of John Kelly of Killann – later the home of the celebrated Rackard brothers, the great Wexford hurlers. The late nineteenth century witnessed the creation of a whole new generation of '98 songs – notably by P. J. McCall. His stirring anthems "Boolavogue" and "Kelly the boy from Killann" displaced the original '98 ballads like "At Monaseed on a summer's morning" from the Wexford repertoire. The maudlin later version of "The Croppy Boy" displaced the haunting original. These Victorian confections now dominate the popular repertoire on 1798.

Private Collection

The Kayle Mummers

Kavanagh's sectarian version so dominated Wexford opinion that it may have repressed and redefined the folk tradition of '98. The mummers' rhymes were rewritten by a Bree schoolmaster called Sinnott to reflect this new version of 1798. The rhymes feature Fr Murphy, Michael Dwyer and John Kelly, alongside Lord Edward, Wolfe Tone and Robert Emmet. These displaced the earlier figures like Saint George. This 1930s photograph is of the Kayle mummers in county Wexford.

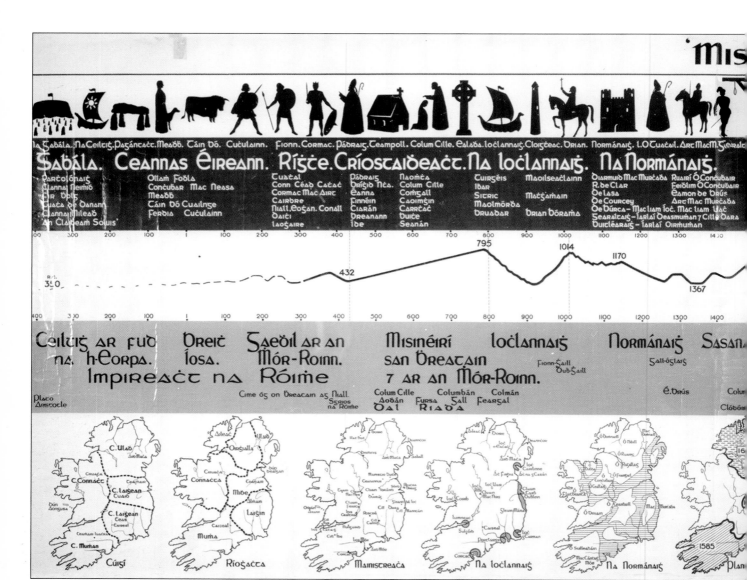

Mise Éire

In the nationalist version of 1798, the rebellion was also absorbed into a narrative of the onward march of the Irish nation towards independence. In this 1940s teaching aid, a timeline of Irish history records the highs and lows. 1798 figures as the highpoint of the eighteenth century which also initiates an unstoppable momentum towards the achievement of the state. The highlight of Irish history is not reached until 1932 – when the Eucharistic Congress affirmed the Catholic ethos of the new state.

Francis Joseph Bigger

This partisan confiscation of the memory of 1798 by the Catholics erased a distinguished moment in the history of Irish Presbyterianism. Some Presbyterians continued to revere the memory of 1798. Francis Joseph Bigger, editor of the *Ulster Journal of Archaeology*, was an indefatigable chronicler of the Presbyterian United Irishmen.

'Éire'

ÓR

Froude and Lecky

1798 remained a historiographical battlefield throughout the nineteenth century. The set-piece confrontation was between J. A. Froude and W. H. Lecky. The imperialist and racist Froude presented the old Protestant version of 1798 derived from Musgrave with an additional racial tinge ('98 as a battle between Celts and Saxons). Lecky, a liberal Unionist and a trained archival historian, devoted a considerable portion of his five-volume history of eighteenth-century Ireland to the 1790s, demolishing Froude and presenting the first modern narrative of the period.

Private Collection

129

Sydney Owenson (Lady Morgan) by René Berthon

She was sympathetic to the United Irishmen and their cultural project and portrayed them favourably in her 1806 novel *The Wild Irish Girl.*

N.G.I.

Novels on 1798

As with the historians, novelists were transfixed by '98 in the nineteenth century. Over 100 novels dealt with the period, culminating in a deluge in the centenary decade of the 1890s. As the Home Rule crisis intensified, obsessive attention was focused on the Act of Union and on the rebellion which precipitated it.

"Our poor Emmet hanging so recently in the street, does not suffer us to enjoy our miseries in any fiction for years to come."

(Lady Charleville to Sydney Owenson)

Maria Edgeworth

Maria Edgeworth was more ambiguous than Lady Morgan. Writing from within an Irish whig tradition, she condemned the United Irishmen but attacked with equal vehemence the stupidity and cruelty of the irresponsible Irish landed class, whose sanguinary, shortsighted policies precipitated the rebellion.

"You may track Ireland through the statute-book of England, as a wounded man in a crowd is tracked by his blood."

(Thomas Moore)

"Though I saw him but this once, his peculiar dress, the elastic lightness of his step, his fresh, healthful complexion and the soft expression given to his eyes by their long dark eyelashes, are as present and familiar to my memory as if I had intimately known him. Little did I then think that at an interval of four-and-thirty years from thence, I should not only find myself the historian of his mournful fate, but (what to many will appear matter rather of shame than of boast) with feelings so little altered, either as to himself or to his cause."

(Thomas Moore on Lord Edward Fitzgerald)

William Carleton

N.G.I.

Thomas Moore

So often dismissed as a lightweight snob (who "turned the wild harp of Erin into a musical snuff box" and who "dearly loved a lord"), he remained a life-long defender of the United Irishmen. His 1831 *Life of Lord Edward Fitzgerald* was a courageous work as was his satirical masterpiece *Memoirs of Captain Rock*. Moore's poetry is suffused with United Irish themes; his recurrent use of light and darkness refers to the United Irish project and its defeat.

John Banim

A Kilkenny O'Connellite, he sought to distance respectable middle-class Catholics from any complicity in the rising in his *The Croppy*.

"The light of 1782 soon passed away and left in the hearts of those who loved Ireland only a vague and restless imagination of what she might have been."

(Thomas Moore)

**Father Michael Murphy
Ceramic Plaque, 1898**

Arrah na Pogue **Playbill** *c.*1898

The most popular Irish Victorian dramatist, Dion Boucicault, wrote many melodramas about the rebellion.

1798.
THE DEATH OF FATHER MICHAEL MURPHY.

PETER: Did you see an old woman going down the path?

PATRICK: I did not, but I saw a young girl, and she had the walk of a queen.

(W.B. Yeats, *Cathleen Ni Houlihan*)

Bold Robert Emmet

The culmination of this literary tradition of 1798 was William Butler Yeats's play *Cathleen Ni Houlihan* (1902) set against the backdrop of the French landing in Killala. Yeats was London chairman of the Centenary Committee. Maud Gonne played the lead role and electrified Dublin audiences when she came on stage at the end of the play. It seemed as if the spirit of '98 was reincarnated in a thrilling way. Yeats was to agonise after 1916 about the play's potent appeal to young nationalists:

Did that play of mine send out certain men the English shot?

In this welter of writing, lavish attention was focused on Lord Edward and "Bold Robert Emmet, the darling of Erin" as prototypes of the selfless Protestant nationalist and as none too subtle role models for the Unionist population. The Emmet legend inspired countless poems, plays and ballads, the best of which was Moore's "She is far from the land where her young hero sleeps".

William Butler Yeats

Emmet as Washington

She is far from the land where her young hero sleeps,
And Lovers are round her, sighing:
But coldly she turns from their gaze, and weeps,
For her heart in his grave is lying.

She sings the wild song of her dear native plains,
Every note which he lov'd awaking; —
Ah! little they think who delight in her strains,
How the heart of the Minstrel is breaking.

He had liv'd for his love, for his country he died,
They were all that to life had entwin'd him;
Nor soon shall the tears of his country be dried,
Nor long will his love stay behind him.

Oh! Make her a grave where the sunbeams rest,
When they promise a glorious morrow;
They'll shine o'er her sleep, like a smile from the West,
From her own lov'd Island of sorrow.

133

The Women of '98

A Scout of '98. "The Yeos!"

Active images of women were rare in the visualisation of 1798. This one is from the *Weekly Freeman* of 1891.

Anne Devlin

The faithful servant of Robert Emmet – patient, passive, steadfast – was presented as a role model for nationalist women.

The Yeos! The Yeos! After Vinegar Hill

A classic Victorian version of female domesticity disturbed by male military activities. The sleeping dog and baby contrast with the Yeomen furiously ranging the countryside.

The Tone Memorial

Tone from his Death Mask by John Kelly

In the roadway at the head of the street a slab was set to the memory of Wolfe Tone and he remembered having been present with his father at its laying. He remembered with bitterness that scene of tawdry tribute. There were four French delegates in a brake and one, a plump smiling young man, held, wedged on a stick, a card on which were printed the words: Vive l'Irelande.

... Or was the jesuit house extraterritorial and was he walking among aliens? The Ireland of Tone and of Parnell seemed to have receded in space.

(James Joyce, *Portrait of the Artist as a Young Man*)

Maquette of the Tone Memorial

The Irish Republican Brotherhood was at the centre of the organisation of the centenary, with the veteran Fenian John O'Leary as figurehead and the Dublin Methodist Frederick Allan as the principal organiser. After a bitter tussle, the nationalist groups who had split acridly after the Parnell débâcle, finally reached agreement to share a platform. One of the main events was the enormous procession to lay the foundation stone of the Wolfe Tone Monument – quarried on Belfast's Cave Hill. Ironically, the monument itself was never completed but this photograph of the maquette shows its impressive design by John Cassidy of Manchester. The figures include Wolfe Tone, manacled, uttering his famous declaration: "For the cause which I have embraced"; an allegorical winged figure "The Spirit of Patriotism urging the principles of the United Irishmen" typified by Michael Dwyer and Lord Edward Fitzgerald with clasped hands; Henry Joy McCracken at the Battle of Antrim; Father John Murphy at Vinegar Hill; at the rear of the monument, Erin with harp and wolfhound, and arms extended; in her left hand the national standard, in her right the wreath of Victory. The monument was to be built of polished Donegal granite with bronze figures.

N.M.I

John Redmond

Even the initially hostile John Redmond was forced to participate fully in the centenary. Attacked by Fr Kavanagh for the role his paternal grandfather had played as a Catholic yeoman in 1798, Redmond played up his maternal grandfather, William Kearney, a member of the Directory which ran the Wexford Republic in June 1798. Redmond's emphasis on the rebellion was to pinpoint its role in the abolition of his favoured "Grattan's Parliament", a role model for a Home Rule parliament. Redmond also focused on the sordid details of how the Union was passed, in blood money and bribery, thereby undermining the moral and political basis of the Union settlement.

Centenary Membership Cards

These cards were issued to members of the National (top) and the Wicklow commemorative organisations (bottom).

Visualising '98

Scullabogue

Unionists responded to the centenary by erecting a mural of Cruickshank's notorious drawing of Scullabogue. These non-contemporary and entirely fanciful images were constantly recycled by those hostile to the United Irish project.

*"I traced them to the Linen
    Hall stacks –
Munro, Hope, Porter and
    McCracken;
Like sweet yams buried
    deep, these rebel minds
Endure posterity without a
    monument,
Their names a covered
    sheugh, remnants, some
    brackish signs."*

(Tom Paulin, 1987)

'98 on Film

The centenary catapulted 1798 into the popular imagination. In the first quarter of the twentieth century, no fewer than five fiction films were made about the rebellion. This still is from *Rory O'More* (1911), directed by Sidney Olcott.

Irish Film Archive

137

United Irishmen
(by column
top to bottom)

Column 1
Joseph Holt
W. J. MacNevin
Henry Jackson
Samuel Neilson
Oliver Bond

Column 2
Lord E. Fitzgerald
J. Napper Tandy
John Sheares
William Corbett

Column 3
William Orr
T. W. Tone
H. Joy McCracken
Bart. Teeling
Fr John Murphy

Column 4
Arthur O'Connor
Robert Emmet
Michael Dwyer
Thomas Russell

Column 5
A. H. Rowan
T. A. Emmet
Henry Sheares
James Hope
William Aylmer

The Leaders of the United Irishmen

This fine poster was produced in Dublin in 1908.

The Long Memory

"*Kevin O'Higgins' speech on the Flogging Bill in the Free State Senate was received with the warmest and most prolonged out= burst of approval yet heard in either House of the Oireachtas.*"

—"*Irish Times,*" July 27th, 1923.

Just so did the forbears of the Freemason Senators cheer the brutal excesses of the Yeos and ancient Britons in '98.

Bitter Rhetoric

1798 also supplied a political rhetoric as in this 1923 attack on Kevin O'Higgins.

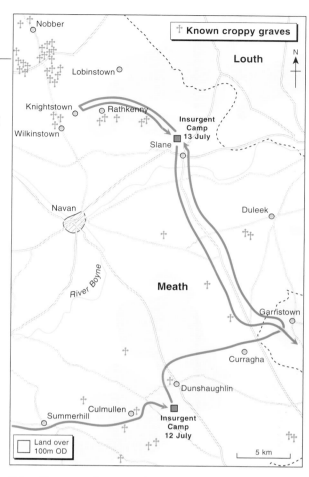

The Croppy Graves of County Meath

The folklore of 1798 lingered long. In a remarkable exercise in the 1930s and 1940s, a Meath-based garda called Murphy painstakingly pinpointed the "croppy graves" of Meath. These were the graves of the Wexford and Wicklow men who had fallen on the incredible long march into Meath.

Clonegal Commemoration 1948

Other commemorations were held in 1938 and 1948 especially in Wexford where they were organised by Michael Kehoe and Fr Patrick Murphy. This photograph shows the schoolchildren of Clonegal in County Carlow marching in the 1948 commemoration.

Requiem for the Croppies

The pockets of our great coats full of barley—
No kitchens on the run, no striking camp—
We moved quick and sudden in our own country.
The priest lay behind ditches with the tramp.
A people, hardly marching—on the hike—
We found new tactics happening each day:
We'd cut through reins and rider with the pike
And stampede cattle into infantry,
Then retreat through hedges where cavalry must be thrown.
Until, on Vinegar Hill, the fatal conclave.
Terraced thousands died, shaking scythes at cannon.
The hillside blushed, soaked in our broken wave.
They buried us without shroud or coffin
And in August the barley grew up out of the grave.

Croppy Poppies

The Croppies

Seamus Heaney wrote a famous poem "Requiem for the Croppies" in the 1960s. One of the best known poems about the period, it is still couched essentially within the Catholic–nationalist paradigm, which presents the Wexford rebels in Fr Kavanagh's terms as depoliticised peasants. Ironically, it was not barley but poppies that sprouted on Vinegar Hill the year after the Battle. The broken thin soil on the hill encouraged a massive flowering of these "Croppy Poppies" which literally turned the hillside red.

Seamus Heaney
by Edward McGuire

Enniscorthy Commemorations

Private Collection

1938 Commemoration at Enniscorthy

The centenary celebrations were so successful in County Wexford that an enormous enthusiasm was generated. Vinegar Hill became indelibly associated with the county and the iconography of Enniscorthy. In 1938 this enthusiasm was still evident in the large crowds attending the events organised by Fr Pat Murphy of Glynn, County Wexford. So thoroughly did he become immersed in the rebellion that he was universally known by the nickname "'98".

Private Collection

Billy Rackard

In 1989 a major Bastille Day celebration was held in Enniscorthy to mark the influence of the French Revolution on Ireland. The great Wexford hurler, Billy Rackard, represented "Kelly the boy from Killann" as his equally famous brother Nicky had done in 1948. The Rackards were reared in the ancestral home of John Kelly in Killann and grew up steeped in the lore of '98. To the present day, 1798 remains an enduring element of the personality of County Wexford.

The Materiality of Memory: Objects from the 1798 Exhibition

"The struggle of memory against forgetting"

"Images and objects signify common loyalties and are recognised as emblems of a symbolic past which also claims to be the historical past. These emblems and objects guarantee our own way of feeling about ourselves and as a group and as such they have a potent influence upon our everyday attitudes."

(Seamus Heaney)

"The struggle for power is the struggle of memory against forgetting."

(Milan Kundera)

"1798 is of no more practical use than 1916."

(Edna Longley)

While the various visual and narrative treatments of 1798 have operated very much under the insistent pressure of the present, the physical objects which deal with the period retain the perfect memory of materiality. These objects are, therefore, of the highest possible evidential value and need to be incorporated into any judicious historical assessment of the period.

These objects range from pikes, muskets and daggers to flags and banners, to death masks and medals. Poignantly, those associated with Theobald Wolfe Tone are displayed in the very building – now called Collins Barracks – where he spent his last days on earth as a prisoner.

While this book concerns the past, it is inescapably a product of the present. It is memory which ties past and present together dynamically. But as the great United Irishman James Hope observed towards the close of his life in 1846: "History is only important while it is being made: what matters most is what you do today and tomorrow."

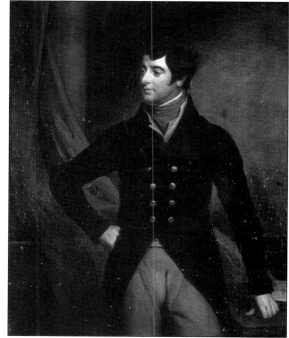

Lord Edward Fitzgerald by Hugh Douglas Hamilton

Irish enthusiasts of the French Revolution were many. The most famous was Lord Edward Fitzgerald, glamorous heir of the Geraldine mantle. In Paris during the Revolution, he warmly endorsed it, becoming friendly with Thomas Paine and other radical *émigrés*. Hugh Douglas Hamilton's portrait of the 1790s shows Edward with fashionably democratic cropped hair, and ostentatiously flaunting a Republican red cravat.

N.G.I.

Lord Edward Fitzgerald

143

Volunteer Tray and Detail

Milltown Fuzileers
Medal

Adare Volunteers
Medal

Volunteer Uniform

Volunteer Jug
and Detail

John Foster Medal

Wedgewood Anti-Slavery Plate

Antrim Militia Uniform

**Ennis Yeomanry
Helmet**

**James Hope's
Bible**

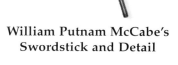

**William Putnam McCabe's
Swordstick and Detail**

Quilt made at Fardystown in County Wexford by women of the Browne Family, 1798

Uniform of the 1782 Club *c.* 1840

Membership Booklet of the Tone Monument Committee

T. Bartlett (ed.), *Life of Theobald Wolfe Tone* (Dublin, 1998).

N. Curtin, *The United Irishmen: Popular politics in Ulster and Dublin 1791-1798* (Oxford, 1994).

D. Dickson, D. Keogh and K. Whelan (ed.), *The United Irishmen: Radicalism, republicanism and rebellion* (Dublin, 1993).

M. Elliot, *Partners in revolution: The United Irishmen and France* (New Haven, 1982).

N. Furlong, *Fr John Murphy of Boolavogue 1751-1798* (Dublin, 1991).

R. Hayes, *The last invasion of Ireland* (Dublin, 1937).

D. Keogh, *The French disease: The Catholic church and radicalism in Ireland 1780-1800* (Dublin, 1993).

D. Keogh and N. Furlong (ed.), *The mighty wave: The 1798 rebellion in Wexford* (Dublin, 1996).

D. Keogh and N. Furlong (ed.), *The women of 1798* (Dublin, 1998).

R. R. Madden, *The United Irishmen: Their lives and times*, 3 vols (Dublin, 1842-1846)

M. O'Dea and K. Whelan (ed.), *Nations and nationalisms: France, Britain, Ireland and the eighteenth-century context* (Oxford, 1995).

J. Smyth, *The men of no property: Irish radicalism and popular politics in the late eighteenth century* (Dublin, 1992).

A. T. Q. Stewart, *A deeper silence: The hidden origins of the United Irishmen* (London, 1993).

M. H. Thuente, *The harp restrung: The United Irishmen and the rise of literary nationalism* (Syracuse, 1994).

K. Whelan, *The Tree of Liberty: Radicalism, Catholicism and the construction of Irish identity 1760-1830* (Cork, 1996).

List of Sources

Frontispiece: An Irish Volunteer taking Liberty under his protection, hand-coloured mezzotint by Jean Delatre from a drawing by Stothard, published by Thomas Macklin, London, 1786, N.L.I. H.P. 1798 (42).

Page 1: The Tree of Liberty, emblem of the Government 1798 Commemoration Committee.

Page 2: The Lambeg and Lisburn Volunteers firing a *feu de joie* in the Market Square of Lisburn to celebrate the Dungannon Convention, by John Carey c.1890, chromo-lithograph, N.L.I. H.P. 1798 (47).

Page 3: Paddy's Resource, engraving published Dublin c.1780, N.L.I. Prints and Drawings.

Page 4: Earl of Charlemont, hand-coloured engraving after a painting by H.A. Hone, published by Thomas Nugent, London, 1790, N.L.I. Char-Ja (4), Elmes P.

— George Washington, miniature, N.M.I. 1895-54.

Page 5: The Phoenix or the Resurrection of Freedom by James Barry, 1776, British Museum.

— Self portrait by James Barry, Royal Society of Arts, London.

Page 6: James Napper Tandy, hand coloured engraving c.1784, N.M.I. S.E. 158.

— George Washington, engraving c.1784, N.L.I. Prints and Drawings.

— Cormac Common, fin-sgealaidhe, from a painting by W. Ousely in J.C. Walker, *Historical memoirs of the Irish bards* (Dublin, 1786).

Page 7: Membership certificate of the Hibernian Society of Philadelphia by John James Barralet, Winterthur Museum, U.S.A.

— The Dublin Volunteers on College Green by Francis Wheatley, 1782, N.G.I. 125.

— America a prophecy by William Blake, 1793, Huntington Library, San Marino, California.

Page 8: The bishop in the Suds or the Revd Barber close-shaving Pro Bono Publico, engraving, Dublin, 1787, N.L.I. Prints and Drawings.

Page 9: A.H. Rowan, *Walker's Hibernian Magazine*, February 1794.

— Charlemont, engraving c.1782, N.L.I. Prints and Drawings.

— Henry Grattan from Madden, *United Irishmen*.

Page 10: The Gates of Calais or the Roast Beef of Old England by William Hogarth, 1748, Tate Gallery, London.

Page 12: The Irish House of Commons by Francis Wheatley, oil on canvas, Leeds City Art Gallery.

— The Three Jacks or the Hunt of Erin, *Irish Magazine*, June 1810.

Page 13: The Louth Mower, engraving c.1792, N.L.I. Prints and Drawings.

— John Fitzgibbon as Lord Chancellor, engraving, c.1790, N.L.I. Prints and Drawings.

— The Right Honourable John Foster, Speaker of the House of Commons of Ireland, from a portrait by Gilbert Stuart, engraved by C.H. Hodges, published London,1792, N.L.I. Prints and Drawings.

— The Custom-House *Non-Pareil*, engraving c.1786, Halliday Collection, Royal Irish Academy.

Page 14: The Irish Brigades in the Service of France, Genealogical Office, N.L.I.

— Charles Carroll of Carrollton, by Joshua Reynolds, 1763, oil on canvas, Mellon Art Gallery, New Haven, Connecticut.

— Richard Hennessy of Cognac, courtesy of Remy-Martin.

— Student at Salamanca, engraving, N.L.I. Prints and Drawings.

Page 15: Philoctetes on the Island of Lemnos by James Barry, 1770, Pinacoteca Nazionale, Bologna.

— Ulysses and a Companion Fleeing the Cave of Polyphemus by James Barry, 1776, Crawford Gallery, Cork.

— Edmund Burke (after G. Romney, 1776), mezzotint, London 1790, N.L.I. Prints and Drawings.

Page 16: Old Burras chapel from Bernard Scalé, The Manor of Castletown in the Barony of Upper Ossory in Queen's County, 1776, uncatalogued manuscript, N.L.I.

— Hedge school, Ballycoris county Mayo, interleaved in N.L.I. copy, C.R. Browne and A.C. Haddon, *The ethnography of the Mullet*.

— A View of the Principal front of the Parliament House and part of the College in Dublin, design'd and drawn by Sir Ed. Pierce, ink and wash, N.L.I. Prints and Drawings, 589TB.

Page 17: The Harvest Dance at Rosanna by Maria Spilsbury Taylor, private collection.

— The Rightboys Paying their Tithes 1785-1786, Bennett Ms 4161, N.L.I.

Page 18: Rathronan House, Mulrankin, County Wexford, photograph by Tomás Hayes.

Page 19: Going to Mass, engraving, N.L.I. Prints and Drawings.

Page 20: The conquerors of the Bastille by Hippolyte Delaroche, Musée Carnavalet, Paris.

Page 22: Volunteer Demonstration in Belfast in 1793, in Honour of the Destruction of the Bastille, by John Carey, in *Ulster Journal of Archaeology*, iv (1897), p. 85.

— *Songs of the French Revolution* (Belfast, 1792).

— The Edgeworth family by Adam Buck, lithograph, N.G.I. 11,508.

Page 23: The unfortunate Theobald Wolfe Tone, *Walker's Hibernian Magazine*, October 1798.

Page 24: T.W. Tone, oil on canvas, N.G.I. 1784.

— S. Neilson, engraving by T.W. Huffam, after a miniature by Charles Byrne, in Madden, *United Irishmen*.

— T. Russell, *Walker's Hibernian Magazine*, October 1803.

— W. Drennan, engraving by T.W. Huffam, from original in Ulster Museum, in Madden, *United Irishmen*.

— O. Bond, miniature, N.M.I. HH 1936-136A.

— J. Hope, engraving by T.W. Huffam, from original in Ulster Museum, in Madden, *United Irishmen*.

— R. Dry, courtesy of Jenny Mayne, Christchurch, New Zealand.

— A.H. Rowan, *Walker's Hibernian Magazine*, February 1794.

Page 25: Anti-Slavery plate, ivory, metal and watercolour, N.G.I. 3722.

Page 26: *Children's Catechism*, Joy Ms., Linen Hall Library, Belfast.

— A National Volunteer, *Walker's Hibernian Magazine*, July 1792.

Page 27: Four Towns Bookclub, *Ulster Journal of Archaeology*, vii (1902), p.102.

— Cork manuscript, R.I.A. Ms. 3-B-46.

Page 28: Storming the Bastille, engraving, published Paris, 1789, N.L.I. Joly Collection.

Page 28: The Modern Beheading Machine at Paris, engraving, published London, 1793.

156

Index

Works of art and literature are presented in italics.